Stand out
with your
scientific poster

Toon Verlinden & Hans Van de Water

STAND OUT
with your
scientific
POSTER

A step by step approach

ACADEMIA
PRESS

Academia Press
Coupure Rechts 88
9000 Gent
België

www.academiapress.be

Academia Press is a subsidiary of Lannoo Publishers.

ISBN 9789401497800
D/2024/45/201
NUR 810

Toon Verlinden & Hans Van de Water
Stand out with your scientific poster. A step by step approach
Gent, Academia Press, 2024, 176 p.

Design: Armée de Verre Bookdesign

CONTENTS

PART 2: Attention **63**

PART 3: At the conference **149**

A SHORT SUMMARY

14 steps to a good poster

QUICK REMINDERS

→ **In many cases, a pitch poster is better than an expert poster**
Whenever it might be difficult to read your poster or you have an audience that isn't full of experts, you're best off choosing a pitch poster instead of a more standard expert poster. Like, for example, during an online conference, shotgun presentation, research day or a general conference with researchers from various disciplines. We talk more about pitch posters on page 90.

→ **Word count**
Limit the number of words on your expert poster to 400, roughly split between:
→ 140–240 words for your title, intro and conclusions
→ 260–300 words for your body text

A pitch poster typically has 150–200 words.

→ **Font size**
→ **Readable from roughly 3 metres**
Title: 96 pt (or for a short title: 120 pt)
Subtitle: 60 pt
→ **Readable from roughly 1.5 metres**
Headers: 50 pt
Body text: 32–40 pt
→ **Readable from roughly 40 cm**
At least 24 pt. Note that this is the *minimum* font size for e.g. references. Body text needs to be bigger.

→ **Check the dimensions and orientation** before you start creating your poster in a design tool. A0 and A1 are the most common sizes.
  → A0: 118.9 cm x 84.1 cm
  → A1: 84.1 cm x 59.4 cm

→ **Don't forget your contact info**

Intro

Congratulations. It's a poster!

You've been selected to present your research in the form of a scientific poster. Congratulations! Something to smile about, and rightly so. A poster fair is a place where you'll have interesting conversations, meet new people and gain some fascinating insights. Who knows, you may even get some valuable feedback from that all-important expert as well. Or at least... that's what it should be like.

In reality, a poster fair is often quite challenging. On the one hand, you have the researcher standing enthusiastically next to their poster, but after a while realising that visitors are avoiding eye contact and that nobody wants to talk. On the other hand, you have the participating researcher who's bravely searching for new insights and developments but ends up rushing around between walls of poster text that have been expertly written in abstract sentences full of jargon. At the end, both the researcher and the visitor are left with a bad feeling. That poster fair had so much potential, so what went wrong?

As you read that last paragraph, your mind may have been darting in all directions: how do you make a good poster then? Is a poster session useful? What if nobody comes to talk to you and you're bored out of your mind as you fidget awkwardly next to your poster panel? All valid questions, because if you don't take the right approach with your poster, it's guaranteed to get lost in a sea of all the other posters at the conference. But there's an extra challenge: as well as standing out from the crowd, your poster also needs to be more appealing than the coffee break.

It's no secret that conferences often organise their poster sessions to coincide with the breaks. The audience has just sat through four presentations in a row and can now finally stretch their legs. They're on their way to the coffee break to catch up with their colleagues, but on the way there they come across you and your poster. At that point, you need to convince them not to take that well-earned break, but to listen to you and look at your poster instead. And to win that battle, you're going to need a solid argument.

Don't get me wrong, a poster fair is a fantastic event. A celebration of science. Together with presentations and papers, posters are the most important way for researchers to communicate with each other. But unfortunately, the way we make posters actually prevents conversations from getting started during the fair and visitors from taking home insights. And that's a shame. To get the most out of a poster fair, scientific posters need to be a lot better.

The *real* goal of a poster: getting conversations started

Why are you making a poster? Why are you investing time and money in presenting it at a conference? Of course, a few days at a conference in New York, Barcelona or Cape Town doesn't sound bad, and getting to 'play tourist' is a bonus, but it's not the reason you take your poster to a conference.

Perhaps you think you're making a poster to convey information. To explain to other people what you did during your research and show the results you've already found. But presentations and papers do a much better job of conveying information. When it comes to papers and presentations, your audience can sit down and quietly process the information. And it's one-way traffic: you explain or write everything down; they listen or read and can take notes.

In that respect, a poster is in fact completely useless for conveying information. Your audience is standing in a busy conference hall; people are staring at them as they walk around; they're short on time; it's not so easy for them to take notes; and if there's too much information on your poster, they'll completely ignore it.

During a poster fair, your audience is simply not prepared to absorb large amounts of information. They have an hour to walk around a hundred posters and will give you five minutes of their time *at most*. Try conveying enough information *and* having a meaningful conversation in that small space of time. 'Conveying information' is, therefore, at most a nice-to-have for a scientific poster, but it cannot and should not be your main goal.

The *real* goal of your scientific poster is to start a conversation. Because that's where posters come into their own. They are real conversation starters that draw people into the world of your research. You get one-on-one contact with those who stop at your poster, which means an opportunity for a real conversation. You can delve deeper into the questions that your research raises and look for a link to the other persons research. You can share anecdotes, brainstorm follow-up research together, consider where your results can be put to good use, which projects you might be able to start up or which other perspectives would add even more value. A presentation or paper doesn't even come close to doing that. Researchers sometimes see scientific posters as the conference presentation's less important little brother, but that's unfair. A poster is a powerhouse when it comes to conversations and new insights.

That observation provides us with a key takeaway: **the winning poster isn't the one that conveys the most information but the one that starts the most conversations.**

Key takeaway

Posters are for starting conversations, not conveying information.

————

So everything about your poster presentation should be aimed at breaking the ice, starting conversations, and raising questions and interesting insights to be discussed with your fellow researchers. Having information on your poster is of course important, but it's only there to keep the conversation going. To help you answer questions and support your insights with your data. The goal is not to dump all the information from your research on your poster and your audience. In fact, that's a really bad idea.

This single insight will hopefully have a big impact on how you both look at and create posters.

Why do all scientific posters look the same?

————

If you type 'research poster' into a search engine, you'll see posters that all look the same. How did that happen? Why does it feel like a poster has to be an impenetrable wall of text? Simple: because we copy each other and are too afraid to do anything different.

Here's a scenario. Two to three weeks before the conference, you suddenly remember that you really should make a start on that poster. You open up PowerPoint and admit that you actually have no idea where to begin. Posters are a visual medium, and nobody ever taught you how to make one. So you wander down the corridor of your research group and look at the posters hanging on the walls. Or you ask another researcher who has made posters in the past.

That researcher is happy to send you the template they used for their last poster session. It's a template they got from another researcher, who in turn based it on a template from another researcher, who in turn... and so on and so forth, all the way back to the beginning of the poster era, somewhere in the 1970s.

The exact origins of the scientific poster are a bit hazy, but the concept first popped up in Europe, where, because people speak different languages, posters were a useful way for non-native speakers to talk about their research to an international audience.

One of the first mentions of a poster session, from an article in the journal Science, on the 28th of June 1974. Posters 'made their first appearance at a major U.S. meeting in Minneapolis at the Biochemistry/Biophysics Meeting in 1974.' The article also says that poster sessions first appeared in Europe shortly before.

We've been presenting scientific posters for 50 years and for just as long we've been looking to each other for how to make a poster. Nobody knows why we ever decided that science posters had to

Intro

look this way, and they haven't changed since those early years. Let that sink in for a moment: mankind had only just taken its first steps on the moon, and it would still be years before the internet would come along. That's how long ago the first posters were created, and since then hardly anything has changed.

This is how the NASA website looked in 1994.

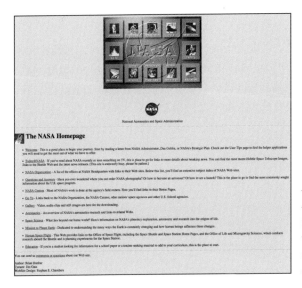

The NASA homepage from 1994. Fortunately, it looks different today. Why do posters still use the same approach even 50 years on?

Can you imagine if it still looked like this now? Of course not. But that *is* the case with scientific posters. A poster from the 1990s is almost indistinguishable from a recent one. There has been no evolution, and that's crazy because a bad scientific poster is a big investment of time and money without giving you much in return, except maybe a mention on your CV. And yet we continue to flock to conferences with posters that are very poor at getting conversations started.

But this rigidity in the poster world also reveals a golden opportunity for you: making a better scientific poster really isn't that difficult. In fact, making a good poster doesn't take any more time and is no more difficult than making a bad one. You just need a different approach.

How your audience reads a scientific poster

Creating a good scientific poster starts with understanding how people read posters. At the start of a poster fair, visitors walk around in the same way they would in a supermarket. They scan the environment in a bit of a hurry. If all goes well, they go through the following three steps:

1 **Something grabs their ATTENTION.** On their quick tour of the poster fair, they'll only stop if something grabs their attention. Typically, this is a clear title, a big image or an eye-catching graph.
2 **They develop an INTEREST.** They keep a safe distance of about three metres because they're not ready to talk to you yet, but they do scan the poster. They read the headers and try to understand the poster's key message.
3 **Their ENTHUSIASM rises.** They move closer and start reading the smaller text or talking to you. This is the moment for you to engage in a real conversation.

Attention–interest–enthusiasm. That order already teaches us a few important things that we'll discuss in more detail later on in the book:

1 **Grabbing someone's attention is extremely important.** If nothing grabs their attention, there's no reason for them to

sacrifice precious minutes on your poster. At this stage, the quality of your research doesn't matter. You may have found both a cure for cancer and a solution to the climate crisis, but if nothing grabs their attention, they won't stop at your poster. (Well, if you cure cancer and solve the climate crisis at the same time, you'll win three or four Nobel Prizes, and everyone will want to talk to you regardless of what your poster looks like. But you get the point.)

2 **People scan a poster before they read it.** From around two or three metres away, they look at the poster for about 10 seconds before deciding whether they're interested. So a poster needs to be as easy to scan as possible. From a distance, people need to be able to quickly scan and understand the titles, graphs and key message you want to convey. It also helps to put keywords in bold and leave enough white space on your poster.

3 **The clock is ticking. Ensure people can read your poster quickly.** Your audience will walk away from posters that look like a paper with two thousand words crammed onto it. That's the moment they realise it would take too much time to analyse it, time that's in short supply at a conference. Sometimes you'll find someone who is extremely interested in your research and willing to spend a long time reading your poster, but those are the exceptions. So it's best to avoid:

→ **Long and difficult titles**
→ **Jargon**
→ **A poster that's hard to scan**
→ **Big blocks of text**
→ **Complicated graphs**

And the list doesn't end there. The more painless it is for your audience to analyse your poster, the more likely they are to read on. Too much or too difficult information will mean they skip your poster and move on to somebody else's.

Key takeaway

A poster that's difficult to analyse combined with a lack of time means that people will skip your poster.

———

How do you make a poster that will get your audience excited? This book aims to provide an answer to that question. Step by step, we'll help you create a poster that has real impact. A poster that quickly provides key takeaways, that stands out from the crowd, and that ensures meaningful conversations and a successful experience. Let's get started!

This book is divided into three parts:

———

1 **CONTENT:** How do you construct a coherent poster and a clear story? What should you put on your poster? And most importantly: what should you leave out?

2 **ATTENTION:** How do you create a poster that is fascinating to look at and that also attracts attention? We'll consider titles, images and how to visualise data, but also some of the less obvious things.

3 **AT THE CONFERENCE:** How should you behave during the conference? What can you do while you're there to increase your chances of success?

Is this the perfect poster?

This book contains lots of examples of scientific posters. Are they all perfect posters? No. But each one is an example of how to apply a certain tip. There is still room for improvement with each poster, but by showing real posters by real researchers, we reveal what is achievable with sometimes just a few small changes. See them as inspiration!

PART 1
Content

Part 1 **Table of contents**

Step 1. Who are you making the poster for?

If you make a poster with the title 'Ecology of the European hamster in the Netherlands', you're going to attract three types of audiences: people interested in ecology, people interested in hamsters, and people from the Netherlands. Each group is looking for different information or reading your poster for a different reason.

Everything depends on who your audience is. People are very quick to realise that they're not interested in something. So your first task is to find out who your audience is and what they are looking for.

The title of the event itself should already be a giveaway. But if it's not clear who the audience is, don't hesitate to ask the organisers. At most events, you'll come across a mixed audience. There will be people who are experts in your domain and people who aren't. With a mixed audience, you have to ask yourself what *you* want to achieve. Do you want to reach as many people as possible? Gain interesting insights from other areas of research? Then you're best off with a poster that everyone understands. But what if you only want to reach people who already know exactly what a *pseudotyped vesicular stomatitis virus* is? That's a valid goal, too, but understand that you'll lose a lot of your potential audience and have a lot fewer conversations.

Don't make the mistake of assuming that every researcher at the conference will know what you're talking about. Conferences can sometimes be very general. If you're at a conference on climate change, for example, there may be researchers working on carbon capture, but also biologists working on biodiversity or social scientists studying migration patterns. So if your poster is a deep dive into carbon capture, you'll lose a large part of your audience.

A common pitfall is showing your poster design to your supervisor to get feedback. There's a good chance they'll want to add extra info and delve even deeper, to really show the world how good your research is. But your poster isn't meant for your supervisor, who already knows your research inside out. At a conference you want to appeal to a new audience that doesn't yet have this knowledge. So when working on your poster, don't start from the question 'What will my supervisor think of this?' but rather 'Will my target audience find this interesting?'

To form a clear picture of your target audience, ask the following three questions:

1 **What do they care about?**
   You may have a clear goal in mind, but the audience will only be interested in your work if you have something to offer them. Instead of using your poster to provide the standard overview of everything you did in your research, ask yourself what message your target audience is interested in.

Choose a message that's tailored to the specific audience.
This means that copy-pasting what you used at a previous conference isn't an option. Find out in advance who will be there
and what you can do for them. The more you have to offer them,
the more open they'll be to talking. If the audience for your
European hamster research is mainly interested in how many
hamsters there still are in the Netherlands, there's little point in
doing a deep dive into the methods you used to investigate the
microbiology of their intestines.

2 **What do they already know?**
Now you know what your audience cares about, you may won-
der how deep you can go. Not everyone wants to do a deep dive
into your research. A general overview of your work, supplemented with the key takeaways, is usually more than enough. **So
always start with something your audience already knows,
then build on that one step at a time.** If you dive straight into
concepts that are new to them, they'll quickly decide they're
not interested. For example, if you work with the material perovskite, resist the temptation to use that as your starting point.
It would be much better to start with the flexible solar panels
that could be made from that material. Try to start from your
audience's knowledge, not from your own.

3 **What jargon do they use?**
If you overload people with words they don't know, they'll
switch off and start frantically searching for the exit. So limit
your jargon. Are you working with monoclonal antibodies to
create a treatment for Ebola, but your audience has no idea
what monoclonal antibodies are? Then just say you're researching a protein to make a treatment for Ebola. If they want to
know exactly which protein you're researching, they'll ask. Or
rather than putting it in the title, you could mention it somewhere lower down on your poster.

Here are some examples of short audience analyses applied to different types of events:

→ **Conference – general:** Most of the audience wants a general overview, doesn't know much about your research and may not be familiar with the jargon you use.

→ **Conference – specific:** The audience mainly wants to know what your methods and results are, and whether they can use or incorporate them too. They may already be familiar with your topic and will probably use the same jargon.

→ **Industry day:** Visitors usually care about feasibility and return on investment of what you're researching. They don't know much about your research and use completely different jargon. They look at it in terms of everyday practicalities and applicability.

→ **General public:** From patients to farmers and from teachers to local residents, 'general public' covers all kinds of people, but typically they want to know what the results are and how they relate to their own lives. They don't know a lot about your topic and don't use jargon.

→ **Departmental research day:** During a research day, researchers from different disciplines drop by. They want to get to know you as a person, hear how you approached your research and whether they can link it to their own project. They've usually heard about your research group but not about your research, and use completely different jargon.

Exercise
Who is your audience? What do they care about, what do they already know and what jargon do they use?

Step 2. Choose one key message

As you're hopefully starting to realise, a poster isn't designed to cram in masses of information. But what message *do* you want to convey with your poster? That message needs to be immediately clear. People will be walking past you quite quickly and should be able to judge in just a few seconds what the key message of your poster is and whether it's relevant for them. If they're interested in that message, they'll stick around. If not, or if they can't grasp the message in around four seconds, they'll carry on walking.

So your key message needs to be clear. And what's more: your key message is just about the only thing your poster needs to convey, supplemented by experiments, data and explanations that support that key message, of course.

Key takeaway

Posters should only convey the key message of your research, not the entire contents of your paper.

A key message might be your most important conclusion or a state-ment about the actions you want to take and could look like this:

→ Between 4 and 25% of nursing home residents struggle with major depression. (conclusion)
→ We need to better understand the impact of extreme tempera-ture events on mortality risks. (statement)
→ The representation of journalists in your favorite Netflix show in-fluences how you think about journalists. (conclusion)

The challenge? Researchers themselves often don't know exactly what their key message is. They describe their research and have some conclusions, but they've never thought about what they want their audience to remember about their poster or do after reading it.

So make sure you yourself are clear about what your key message is. **The best key message is one sentence without any jargon.** It should be a sentence that people understand without needing to read the rest of your poster.

The poster may explain the key message in more detail (in fact, that's the main purpose of your poster), but it's important to realise that those who don't understand your key message won't read the rest of it. Do you want to appeal to as many people as possible at a conference? Then make your key message something that as many people as possible will understand straight away.

The only exception to a key message without jargon is if you're aiming to attract a specific audience. For example, if you're at a conference about dairy, you may want to use a word like 'casein' in your key message. But understand that you're then only going to appeal to people who know what that word means and the rest of the audience won't stop at your poster.

Exercise
Write down your key message in one sentence, without using any jargon.

Put your key message all over your poster

Once you have a key message, it's best to put it on your poster in as many ways as possible. Unfortunately, it feels like a lot of researchers go out of their way to hide their key message as best as they can. Their message is usually somewhere in the bottom right-hand corner of the poster, hidden in the conclusions block. Your audience first has to wade through the entire poster, get to the conclusions block – where there are five different bullet points – and then extract *and* remember the key message from that jumble of words. They're not going to do that.

You can leave the conclusions block as is, but your key message should appear in various other places on your poster so that everyone – whether they look at your poster only briefly or at length – can immediately see what you want to convey.

For example, put your key message in:
→ Your title
→ Your introduction
→ Your results
→ Your images

1. Put your key message in your title

We'll go into titles in more detail in step 8 (page 82), but what's important to know for now is that you're not obliged to put the title of your paper or PhD research at the top of your poster. Instead, you can put your key message in your title or your subtitle.

2. Put your key message in your introduction

Putting your key message in the introduction of your poster, is a really good idea. It might sound crazy to share your key conclusion so brazenly right at the start, but it really does work: after about three sentences everyone knows what you're trying to achieve and can decide whether the poster is relevant for them. Newspaper articles are structured in the same way: the most important information appears in the title and the opening, and the more detailed info comes later.

A lot of researchers find the advice to include your key message in the introduction a bit strange. They're afraid it will 'spoil' their research, that they'll be revealing the best bits too early on. They argue that, in Hollywood, spoilers are a cardinal sin that ruin it for the audience. You don't give away how a film ends, because then nobody would want to come and see it, would they?

Correct. They wouldn't. But your poster is not a Hollywood movie. You need to remember: the job of your poster is to share your key message with your audience. Is your audience going to spend just ten seconds on your poster? Then you'll have to see what you can teach them in ten seconds. The purpose of a film is to entertain us from beginning to end. The purpose of a poster is to convey a key insight so that you can talk about it with each other. It's important that you start talking about your key message as soon as possible and it's okay to give away the most important insight from the start. No spoiler alert required.

Another reason it's best to keep the key message as short and simple as possible and to put it in the introduction, is time. In their native language, people can read around a hundred words a minute on your poster. In another language or if the sentences are full of jargon, that number drops. In the few seconds they spend looking at your poster and deciding if they're interested, they can read at most around ten words in the title plus a few more things. If your key message is easy to find *and* read in the introduction, they'll spend the few remaining words they can read in that short time on the most relevant content.

3. Put your key message in your results

Discuss only experiments, projects or areas of work that relate to your key message. Did you set up an interesting side experiment? Great! But if that side experiment has nothing to do with your key message, take it out. Do you have five graphs and two tables, but only two of the graphs relate to your key message? Then delete the rest.

You can often also express your key message in the title of those graphs by sharing the conclusion that supports your key message. We'll talk more about graphs in step 11, page 126.

4. Find images that support your key message

Find an image that supports your key message. Did you do research into empty lunch boxes and conclude that hot meals at school are the best way to solve this problem? Then put an image of an empty lunch box and a hot meal right in the middle of your poster. We'll discuss images in more detail in step 9 (page 102).

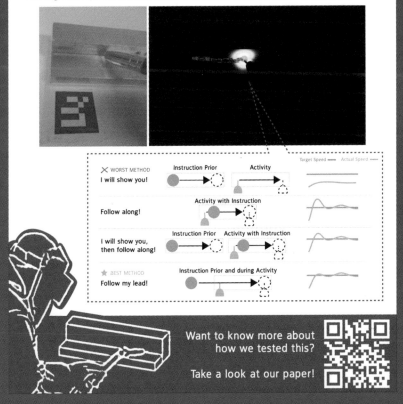

The Art of Timing:

Effects of AR visual guidance timing on speed of movement

Jeroen Ceyssens, Bram Van Deurzen, Gustavo Rovelo Ruiz, Kris Luyten, Fabian Di Fiore
Expertise Centre for Digital Media - Flanders Make, Hasselt University, Belgium

To convey speed, do not just show an example, let them follow!

Activities such as welding are very hard and difficult to learn, causing a lot of errors and costs. We tested guidance for activities using augmented reality, showing instructions at different times. Showing an example is not enough to convey the correct speed, it is best to let them follow.

Want to know more about how we tested this?

Take a look at our paper!

The first thing you see on this poster is the key message in the introduction box: 'To convey speed, do not just show an example, let them follow.' Even if you only look at the poster for ten seconds, you know what the researcher wants to convey. The rest of the poster explains that it's about learning good welding techniques using AR, with a focus on the speed at which you create the weld seam (poster by Jeroen Ceyssens).

Wearables in de strijd tegen
Alzheimer

prijzen
INGENIEURSVERENIGING

2020
Linde Proost

Het potentieel van stress-monitoring in Alzheimer

Wereldwijd lijden meer dan 50 miljoen mensen aan Alzheimer. Dit is een **onomkeerbare**, degeneratieve hersenaandoening waarbij amyloïd-ß eiwitafzettingen en tau-eiwit aggregaten in de hersenen leiden tot neurotoxische effecten. Dit veroorzaakt een **cognitieve en functionele aftakeling** (en uiteindelijk zelfs dood). Ondanks grote wetenschappelijke inspanningen is een behandeling voor deze vreselijke ziekte helaas nog niet in zicht. Daarom focust dit literatuuronderzoek op een eerder **preventieve aanpak m.b.v. wearables**, om zo het leven van toekomstige patiënten toch comfortabeler te maken.

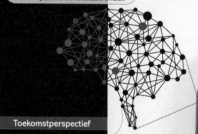

Alzheimer & stress zijn met elkaar gelinkt...

- Uit een uitgebreide literatuurstudie blijkt dat de **locus coeruleus** en de **hippocampus** fysiologisch van groot belang zijn in zowel Alzheimer als de stressrespons.
- Het vermoeden van een link tussen beide processen wordt **bevestigd door eerdere wetenschappelijke publicaties** over de link tussen stress en Alzheimer (zie onderaan).

...via een vicieuze cirkel

Stress verlaagt Alzheimer drempel
Alzheimer pathologie
Amyloïd-ß Tau pathologie Hippocampus atrofie
Verstoring stressrespons
Verhoogd stresshormoon

Conclusie

Stress-monitoring met wearables kan bijdragen aan een **vroegere detectie** en **betere opvolging** van Alzheimer

Toekomstperspectief

Literatuurstudie via PRISMA protocol

Vergelijkende dierproef: verschilt het stresspatroon in gezonde muizen van dat in Alzheimer-muismodellen?

Vergelijkende klinische studie: verschilt het stresspatroon in Alzheimer-patiënten van dat in een gezonde controle-groep?

Lang-lopend experiment: hoe evolueert het stresspatroon van patiënten met een milde, cognitieve stoornis?

Studie naar diagnostisch potentieel: kunnen wearables Alzheimer onderscheiden van andere ziekten?

Lang-lopend experiment: wat is het vroegste teken van Alzheimer detecteerbaar in het stresspatroon?

Voordelen van wearables vs cortisol & vragenlijsten

- Continue monitoring
- Niet-invasief
- Perceptie gelinkt aan objectieve metingen
- Praktisch & goedkoop

Stress-monitoring kan ingezet worden voor:

- **Vroege waarschuwing** voor Alzheimer
- **Opvolging van ziekteprogressie**, vanaf de vroegste stadia
- **Diagnose** van Alzheimer
- **Preventie** of uitstel van Alzheimer

Literatuurstudie: 84-90% bevestigt link tussen stress & Alzheimer

35 klinische studies
26 met Cortisol sampling
22 bevestigen de link
4 ontkennen de link

59 dierproeven
11 met vragenlijsten
10 bevestigen de link
1 ontkent de link

- Eerdere klinische studies a.d.h.v cortisolmetingen en vragenlijsten tonen dat **gestresseerde individuen meer risico** lopen op Alzheimer en dat een **toegenomen hoeveelheid cortisol gelinkt is aan Alzheimer** in een vroeg stadium.
- Eerdere dierproeven bevestigen link tussen stress en: amyloïd-ß, tau-pathologie, verlies aan plasticiteit in de hersensynapsen, degeneratie van de hippocampus en een verlies in cognitieve vaardigheden.

KU LEUVEN VUB VRIJE UNIVERSITEIT BRUSSEL UNIVERSITEIT GENT UHASSELT Universiteit Antwerpen

ie-net
INGENIEURSVERENIGING

KU LEUVEN VBI BEA AIA AIG

The key message 'Stress monitoring through wearables can contribute to earlier detection and better monitoring of Alzheimer's' is right in the middle of the image to grab the audience's attention (poster by Linde Proost).

You can of course also make your key message part of the image it-self. This is a great way to grab the audience's attention. On the left page is a poster in Dutch, but even if you don't speak the language, you can tell that the 'conclusie'-message in the image is important.

Put your key message in BIG letters

A tip: we're increasingly seeing researchers taking the plunge and putting their key message in BIG letters on their poster. This is an excellent idea because it means visitors immediately grasp the key message, even if they only look at your poster for three seconds and from a few metres away.

If you're interested in drones and bees, you'll be instantly drawn to this poster. Note that the key message is an attention-grabbing sentence without jargon, while the title (Using piezoelectric tags and autonomous drone technology to understand the space use of bees at a landscape scale) would immediately put me off (poster by Thomas Oliver).

1 Content

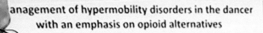

The big text at the top of the poster isn't the title, but the key message. The title is below in smaller, bold letters.

You can also draw extra attention to your key message by simply putting it in a colour or on a coloured background. This doesn't take up any extra space and quickly gets the audience looking in the right place.

Not everyone will want to dedicate a quarter of their poster to their key message, but it's certainly a useful approach that works well. If you're still reluctant to sacrifice so much space for your key message, at least make sure you put it in the title, introduction, results and image.

If you put your key message in all those places, you can be pretty confident that your audience will understand what it's about and remember the essence of it. And if they don't? Then they probably weren't the right audience for your message after all.

But I have several key messages!

Perhaps you have a big project that's divided into five areas of work, each with its own experiments and conclusions. If you want to cover all of these on your poster, you'll notice that you also have five key messages, one for each area of work.

Multiple key messages are a red flag. It usually means you're trying to cram several posters onto one sheet of paper. And that's just making it difficult for yourself. The best thing to do is bring the scope of your poster into focus and zoom in. Don't describe the entire project, but just one area of work, one key message for your poster to focus on. And drop the rest.

One clear message seen by everyone is better than five seen by no one.

Step 3. Write your introduction

Once you know what the focus of your poster is, you can think about the next step: your introduction. There are two introductions that you need to consider: the text that will appear in your poster's introduction block *and* your verbal pitch.

The verbal pitch is the introductory talk you'll have with visitors. Someone will stop at your poster, read the title and a few headers, and look at a graph. That's the moment to get the conversation started with a short pitch about your research to see if they're interested in learning more. Keep your pitch to about a minute, and make sure it covers the most important parts of your research in a clear way yet still leaves them wanting to find out more.

There's a lot riding on the verbal opening pitch, but don't make the mistake of starting the conversation with a five-minute info dump. Nobody has time for that right now. If you do decide to info dump, you'll soon notice the eyes of your audience glazing over. They might be thinking, 'Damn, I actually wanted to go and get a coffee and now I'm stuck here. I didn't ask for this long-winded explanation at all.' At the same time, you're thinking, 'Damn, they're definitely not interested, but I can't really stop talking now, can I?' All in all, an awkward situation that's best avoided for everyone's sake.

It's much better to give a short pitch of about one minute. After that you can judge whether they're interested in hearing more. If they start asking questions and getting excited, they're all ears! You can then dive deeper into your topic and your poster with them.

If after that one minute, you get a short 'Hmm, interesting' but not much else, that's your cue to bring the conversation to a friendly close. They can then go and get their coffee without feeling bad, and you're ready to move on to the next person. There's absolutely nothing wrong with that: everyone has their own areas of interest. I've lost count of the number of times I've found myself standing next to a well-meaning researcher who went the full five minutes. It may not seem like a long time, until you're standing there wanting to look at ten other posters.

The good news? The work you put into that one-minute verbal introduction can simply be reused later for the intro block on your poster.

Your verbal pitch

Read the two pitches below. Warning: the first one doesn't read very well.

Pitch with illogical structure and jargon

→ *This research looks into texture and structure analysis methods of meat and meat analogues like mechanical testing, Texture Profile Analysis, spectroscopy, NMR and imaging techniques. Furthermore, the advantages and limitations of each texture method are described. Even though the texture characteristics of meat are well documented, dedicated methods used to analyse meat analogues are still limited. The key success factor for meat analogue products is their high similarity in sensory properties compared to meat. This research wants to get more insight into the fibres of meat analogues and the development during thermomechanical processing of meat analogues.*

Notice how difficult it was to read that pitch? Did you skip parts (or even the entire pitch)? On the next page is the same pitch, but with a logical structure and less jargon.

→ *Meat substitutes are becoming more and more important in our diet, but although we have a good understanding of the texture and behaviour of meat, we can't say the same for meat substitutes. This makes it difficult to imitate meat in terms of taste and texture.*

Therefore this research looks at techniques that can monitor the texture and structural properties of meat substitutes during production, so that we can make the next generation of meat substitutes even closer to real meat.

The second pitch is a lot easier to read than the first and encourages you to find out more. That's because the second pitch uses a problem–solution–advantage structure. And you can use the same for your own research.

Here are the five steps to creating a good one-minute pitch:
1   Grab their attention.
2   Describe the problem you want to tackle.
3   Indicate the solution you're researching.
4   Say what the advantage is.
5   Conclude.

Now let's dive a bit deeper into each one.

1   **Grab their attention:** you have to grab your audience's attention somehow. For example, by asking a question, telling a story or sharing an interesting fact. You have to paint a picture.
2   **Describe the problem:** what is the problem you're investigating? Why do you want to solve it? There's always a problem or challenge you want to tackle with your research. If you're doing fundamental research, there may not be a practical problem, but there will be a gap in our knowledge that you want to fill.

3 **Indicate the solution you're researching:** say how you want to tackle the problem or challenge, what your research looks like or what steps you're taking.

4 **Say what the advantage is:** share how the public or society will benefit from your research. Does your research give us a better understanding of the problem? Does it provide data that other researchers can use? Will it lead to a new tool?

5 **Conclude:** ideally, you'll conclude with your key message. Sometimes this overlaps with the advantage you've just described, so be careful not to repeat yourself.

Already identified the five elements for your research? Then glue them together using the words BUT, THEREFORE, SO THAT. Your pitch will then be structured like this:

→ PAINT A PICTURE to grab their attention
→ **(BUT)** problem
→ **(THEREFORE)** solution
→ **(SO THAT)** advantage
→ CONCLUDE WITH KEY MESSAGE

Here's how a full pitch might look:

CASE 1: The pain-free way to identify muscle fibre type

PAINT A PICTURE The average person has 50% fast and 50% slow muscle fibres, but the exact split is different for everyone. Even in the 1970s we could tell whether an athlete was training for the right sport based on their muscle-fibre type. After all, a sprinter needs different muscle fibres compared to a marathon runner.

BUT to identify the muscle fibre type, we need to cut a piece of muscle out of the athlete's leg. Something that neither athletes nor coaches are keen to do.

THEREFORE during my PhD I optimised a pain-free method that involves estimating the muscle-fibre type using a non-invasive MRI scan.

SO THAT we can optimise sports performance in a pain-free way based on muscle potential.

CASE 2: Searching for earthquakes

PAINT A PICTURE In 2004, one of the strongest-ever earthquakes was recorded in Sumatra, Indonesia. The tsunami that followed flooded almost all coastal areas around the Indian Ocean and 250,000 people died. Nobody, not even scientists, had expected an earthquake that bad, because there are no historical documents that mention anything about similar catastrophic events in the region.

BUT written documents only go back a few hundred years, so they don't tell the full story of past earthquakes.

THEREFORE I'm studying the ground beneath our feet, where a history of thousands of years of earthquakes is buried. I do this by examining the bottoms of lakes, soil that is only disturbed by an earthquake.

SO THAT I can find out how often major earthquakes occurred in the past and estimate whether we should expect the next major earthquake in that area within 10, 100 or 1,000 years.

KEY MESSAGE: In short: by studying the bottoms of lakes we learn information about earthquakes that no history book can tell us.

By following this structure, you'll end up with a nice well-defined pitch that you can deliver in under a minute. But make sure you don't rehearse your pitch so much that you sound like a robot spouting out lines. Always remember that you're having a conversation, not giving a presentation. That being said, it makes a lot of sense to have a number of these short introductions up your sleeve, so you can pick and choose depending on the different target groups. If you're at a general conference, for example, make sure you have two: one for the non-experts and one for the experts.

> **Exercise**
> *Write out your verbal pitch in a short sentence, using the words 'but', 'therefore' and 'so that' to glue it all together.*

The introduction on your poster

With the verbal pitch you've just written, you also have everything you need to fill out the introduction block on your poster, although you'll leave out the attention grabber at the start. That's because on the poster it is the title, image or graph that will grab the audience's attention.

In the intro block you put your problem, solution, advantage and key message. You'll probably have to make the sentences a little shorter than in the verbal pitch. And if your key message overlaps with your advantage, don't repeat it.

You can put the words 'problem', 'solution', 'advantage', 'key message' on your poster if you want, but it's not necessary. The most important thing is that you now have an introduction that is clear, quick and easy to read.

CASE 1: The pain-free way to identify muscle fibre type

PROBLEM To identify muscle-fibre type, we need to cut a piece of muscle out of the athlete's leg.

SOLUTION Development of a pain-free method to estimate muscle-fibre type using an MRI scan.

ADVANTAGE/KEY MESSAGE We can now optimise sports performance in a pain-free way based on muscle-fibre type.

CASE 2: Searching for earthquakes

Written documents don't tell the full story of past earthquakes. That's why I'm studying the bottoms of lakes, where thousands of years of earthquake history are buried, so that I can find out how often major earthquakes occurred in the past.

KEY MESSAGE By studying the bottoms of lakes, we learn information about earthquakes that no history book can tell us.

Step 4. Draw a pyramid structure

You now have an idea for your key message and what you want to put in the introduction of your poster, but the rest of your poster is still looking a bit empty. How do you fill it up? What you shouldn't do at this stage is open up your design tool and simply throw your text at the page. There's a good chance you'll end up with an unstructured dump of information. You first need a structure that supports your key message, and you get that by drawing a pyramid structure.

A pyramid structure provides an overview of everything that will appear on your poster.

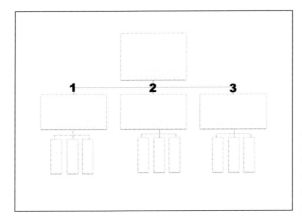

An empty pyramid structure. By filling this out, you get a very clear idea of what you want to put on your poster.

Let's say you need to make a poster about your research into the effect of self-collected samples in the fight against cervical cancer.

The key message of your research is: we need to focus on self-collected samples to screen more people for cervical cancer.

Here is your short pitch: to increase cervical cancer survival rates, it's important that we detect the cancer quickly BUT we're not able to reach 37% of those eligible for cervical cancer screening. They often put off going to a doctor. THEREFORE I'm investigating the effect of self-collected samples like urine samples. These samples are easy to collect and send to the lab yourself, eliminating the need for a doctor's visit. I'm also looking at how we can organise these samples SO THAT we can screen more people for cervical cancer, including those who find it difficult to get to a doctor.

You can draw your pyramid on a computer, but it's often easier on a sheet of paper. Here's how you create your pyramid:

Step 1. Put your key message at the top.

For our example: We need to focus on self-collected samples to screen more people for cervical cancer.

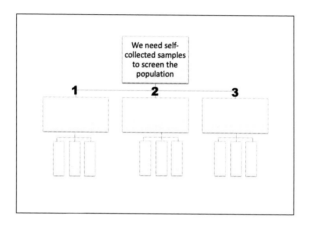

Step 2. Think of up to three things that support your key message.

Put each of those three things in their own box under your key message. They're also the three 'blocks' that – in addition to your introduction and conclusions – will appear on your poster. The three blocks you choose depend on the research you're doing. The example on the next page follows the problem–solution–advantage structure, but you can also use something else. As long as each block is clearly linked to your key message. Are there concepts, results or experiments that you want to explain but aren't really related to your key message? Then they probably don't belong on the poster.

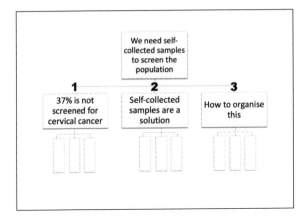

The pyramid you've developed can now be mapped onto the skeleton of our poster as follows:

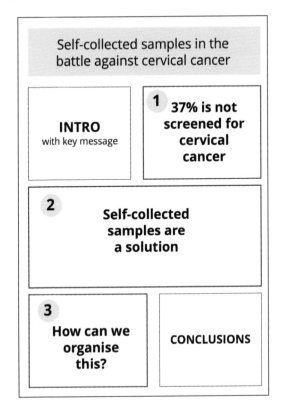

You will probably be able to come up with lots of things to fill those three blocks and it heavily depends on the research you're doing. You might feel inclined to say, 'In the science world, we typically use three blocks: method–results–discussion.' So one possible approach is to fill in the three blocks under your key message with your method, results and discussion, but this is far from ideal. The IMRAD structure (Introduction, Methods, Results And Discussion) was initially developed for scientific papers so it is designed to help people find the right information in 30 pages of text as quickly as possible. And that's good: if information in papers is always in a different place, you would easily spend twice as long on your text analysis.

But posters aren't papers. They contain much less information, and you are standing next to them to guide your audience through the content. So there's no need for the same rigid structure we typically use in papers.

One more thing: look again at your key message. By making the first block a 'method' block, you're indicating that the method is one of the most important things that support your key message. That may be the case if you're researching a new methodology, but the method isn't typically the first thing people want to know. They usually have questions like: why is this such a problem? How are you going to solve this? Why is this useful? In this case, problem–solution–advantage blocks are much more meaningful than method–results–discussion.

Step 3. Flesh out the blocks.

Chosen your three blocks? Then it's time to think about what you actually want to put on your poster. Flesh each block out by indicating where you want to have a graph, for example, or just text. Do you want to illustrate one with a process flow? And another with an image?

In the example below we've fleshed out the first block. We want to explain why it's a problem people don't get screened, and supplement this with a graph showing survival rates and with a few reasons people don't get screened.

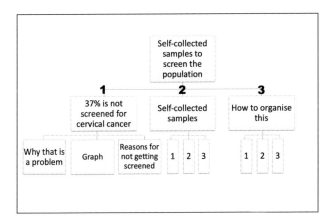

A pyramid structure takes the guesswork out of creating your poster. By thinking about what you want to appear in each block, you'll get a very clear picture of the content of your poster.

In step 5 (page 52) we'll talk about how much text to put on your poster. All you need to know for now is that you can write around 100 words per block. Or 50 words for blocks 1 and 3 and 200 words for block 2, depending on the research.

Often the block where you talk about the solution is longer than the rest. Makes sense: the solution block is about your research. But what if you're only just starting your research? Then your problem and advantage blocks will probably be longer than the solution block. It's up to you to make sure you're happy with how it all fits together.

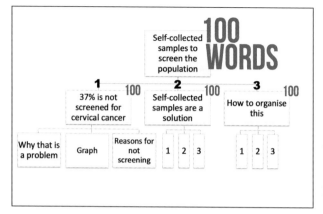

You can put up to 400 words on a poster. This can be split across your structure as in this example.

Exercise

Draw your own pyramid structure. Write your key message at the top and think of three things that support the message. Flesh out that layer with what you actually want to put on your poster.

Step 5. Write your text

Now that you have your structure, you're ready to write your text. But you should still refrain from doing that in your design tool. I recommend first opening up a word processor to type out and polish your text.

When it comes to text, there's one golden rule: **USE LESS TEXT**

Feeling the need to include all their knowledge and findings, researchers often cram their poster full of text. As we mentioned earlier, long texts do NOT work on a poster. During a busy poster fair, your audience simply doesn't have time to read five pages of written text.

A rule of thumb: if your text is clearly written and your poster is well structured, your audience can read around 100 words a minute. That's in the ideal scenario where they're not distracted and can focus their full attention on the poster. A poster with 1,000 words can easily take 10 minutes to read and nobody has time for that at a poster fair.

So, how many words can you put on your poster? Try to limit it to 400 words:
→   140–240 words for your title, intro and conclusions
→   260–300 words for your body text

Key takeaway

Reading 400 words takes around 5 minutes at a busy poster fair. That's typically the maximum amount of time people have.

———

It's always better to use fewer words, but there's also a lower limit that seems to be around 200 words. If you put much fewer than 200 words on your poster, it usually won't be clear enough to understand without you explaining it.

Don't write your 400 words in PowerPoint where it's difficult to count and edit them quickly. Instead, type them out in a word processor and polish them until you're happy. Typed out using a word processor, 400 words is just under a page.

Do you have more than 400 words to say? That's highly likely, but you'll still need to edit it down. If you still feel inclined to include more words on your poster, remember that the purpose of your poster is to start conversations and get your key message across,

1 Content

not to ram as much information as possible down the audience's throat. Give your audience just enough relevant information to follow the story, but no more. So for each piece of text or data, ask yourself whether you really need it.

Fortunately, there's still another option if you want to say more than 400 words: add a QR code or handout with more information. We'll talk more about QR codes and handouts in step 6 on page 57.

> **Exercise**
> *Use a word processor to type out your poster text. Limit it to 400 words.*

Case: The research or the tool?

During a workshop, a researcher told me she wasn't sure which approach to take for her poster. Should she talk about her research, results and experiments? Or specifically about the tool she developed as part of the research? Doing both at the same time would steer her to well over 400 words.

So I asked her, 'What is your goal? Why are you taking your poster to that conference?' Her answer? 'I'd like people to discover and use my tool.' There you have it then: her goal was to promote the tool. So the entire poster needed to focus on that and drop those other experiments and conclusions. If they didn't support the 'you need to try out this tool' message, she had to get rid of them.

Watch out for abbreviations, jargon and project names

Abbreviations are risky business when it comes to posters. You might explain your abbreviation in the introduction, but who's to say people will read your poster in a nice linear way? There's a good chance they'll come across your abbreviation before the explanation, which means they'll struggle to understand your sentence. Best-case scenario, they'll go in search of an explanation, but if that takes too long, they'll lose interest. So use as few abbreviations and acronyms as possible in your text and avoid them in the title or key message.

Jargon is just as dangerous. Your audience reads a sentence they don't understand, looks for an explanation, doesn't find one and concludes that the sandwiches in the break room are more important. Jargon puts people off and forms a textual barrier between your message and your audience. Especially if you're not on hand to explain.

Project names get a special mention. Researchers have a knack for giving their projects cool names, like:

→ SCATMAN (Stroke CAvities Treatment Mechanism with Active Neural interfaces)
→ VAPORE (VApour deposition of crystalline PORous solids)
→ MULTIPLES (The MULTIPLicity of supErnova progenitorS)

You might think there's nothing wrong with that, but project names mean nothing to outsiders. So they don't make sense on a poster. And certainly not in a poster title. Granted, we might be able to make an exception for a pink astrophysics poster with the acronym BARBIE (Bayesian Analysis for Remote Biosignature Identification on exoEarths).

BARBIE

Bayesian Analysis for Remote Biosignature Identification on exoEarths I:
Using Grid-Based Nested Sampling in Coronagraphy Observation Simulations for H₂O

N. Latouf [1,3], A. Mandell[2], G. Villanueva[2], M. Moore[2], N. Susemiehl[2], V. Kofman[2], M. Himes[2]
[1]George Mason University; nlatouf@gmu.edu, [2]NASA Goddard Space Flight Center (GSFC), [3]NSF Graduate Research Fellow

Introduction

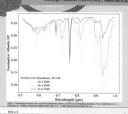

A true Earth-twin analog would occupy the habitable zone (HZ) of a planet such that liquid water can exist at the surface (Kopparapu et al. 2013). Thus, detecting H_2O in an exoplanet atmosphere usually stands as the first step in the search for habitability. These Earth-twins could exhibit a range of H_2O abundances. Multiple factors affect the efficiency of atmospheric characterization at varying wavelengths, including SNR. By prioritizing shorter wavelengths, we can decrease astrophysical noise terms, observe HZs of more distant and lower mass stars, and observe higher photon flux for FGK-type stars. However, H_2O has an increasing number of deep spectral features at longer wavelengths as seen in Figure 1. Therefore, in order to constrain the detectability of H_2O absorption in the spectra of Earth-like atmospheres, we:

- Varied the abundance of H_2O in order to study the impact of central wavelength and detectability as abundance varies through Earth's epochs and changes detectability as a function of wavelength.
- Varied the observational SNR. It is easier to detect H_2O at longer wavelengths with lower SNR, but that works against best telescope operation. Thus, understanding SNR will be crucial to optimize efficient observations.

Here, we present an analysis of detectability of H_2O as a function of abundance and SNR using Bayesian analysis and nested sampling techniques for an Earth-twin analog.

Methods & Results

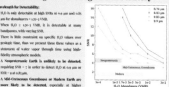

We set a fiducial spectrum from 0.515 – 1 µm split into 25 bandpasses. For abundance case studies, all parameters are kept to modern Earth values except H_2O, which is varied. These inputs are given to the Bayesian retrieval nested sampling routine PSGnest. From the output results file from PSGnest, we calculate the median values, and the 68% credible region. We also calculate the log-Bayes factor to determine detectability:

- if lnB < 2.5, then detection is unconstrained.
- if 5 > lnB > 2.5, then detection is weak.
- if lnB > 5, then detection is strong.

We plot these results as a function of wavelength and investigate how detectability changes as SNR increases in Figure 2.

Minimum H₂O Bandpasses & Multi-Species Constraints:

- H_2O is strongly detectable at all SNR ≥ 2 and weakly detectable at all SNR at wavelengths centered on 0.9 µm.
- H_2O is strongly detectable at 0.72 µm at SNR ≥ 12. This is also the wavelength at which the correct abundance of H_2O is retrieved. At longer wavelengths, the retrieved abundance is overestimated due to a degeneracy with pressure.
- Included the preliminary retrieved Modern Earth abundance of O_2, initial results suggest that at an SNR of 10, a strong detection of both H_2O and O_2 is possible at 0.83 µm.
- By increasing SNR to 12, a strong detection of both H_2O and O_2 is possible at 0.74 µm, at which point the correct abundance of H_2O is retrieved.

Detecting H2O Through Earth's History

Wavelength for Detectability:

- H_2O is only detectable at high SNRs at 0.9 µm and 0.85 µm for abundances < 1.2e-3 VMR.
- When H_2O > 1.2e-3 VMR, it is detectable at many bandpasses, with varying SNR.
- There is little constraint on specific H_2O values over geologic time, thus we present these these values as a statement of water vapor through time using high-fidelity atmospheric models.
- A Neoproterozoic Earth is unlikely to be detected, requiring SNR = 7 in order to detect H_2O at 0.9 µm or SNR = 9 at 0.85 µm.
- A Mid-Cretaceous Greenhouse or Modern Earth are more likely to be detected, especially at higher abundances with mid to low SNRs.

Final Conclusions

- H_2O can be detected down to 0.74 µm with moderate-SNR data for abundances at the upper end of Earth's presumed historical values.
- H_2O can be detected at 0.9 µm with low-SNR data at modern Earth abundances of H_2O.
- By understanding the SNR requirements for detecting molecules of interest and properly prioritizing spectral bandpasses for optimal detectability, we can inform the best instrument designs and observing procedure.

In future work, we will present a similar molecular abundance study for the O_2, O_3 and other potential molecular species that could be present in Earth-twin atmospheres and expand on the trade space in choosing bandpasses for some or all these species. We also plan to build a new, more thorough grid extending to longer wavelengths and adding the additional molecular species. We also intend to make all detectability information available through a PSG module.

References & Acknowledgements

BARBIE is an exception we'll allow to the advice not to use acronyms. Researcher Natasha Latouf received positive international feedback on this design and told us she likes 'to encourage scientists to get creative and have fun with acronyms and designs.'

Step 6. Make a handout and QR code

You may find it difficult to limit the amount of text on your poster. For example, what do you do with references? What about that table that you don't really need but the expert may ask about? Or the abstract or that extra bit of text you should really delete but don't want to? One answer: put them in a handout.

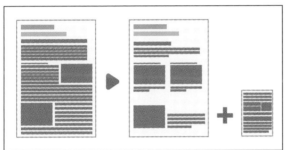

On your poster, put only the essential information that's needed to understand your research and story. Move the rest to a paper or digital handout for people who want to know more.

A handout is the best way to remove things from your poster. Include everything that's too detailed for the average visitor and give it to those who want to know more. You can also keep hold of one of your handouts in case you need an extra graph or table to support your explanation.

This leaves your poster to do what it does best: convey the key message and start conversations. The handout then takes care of communicating information.

You could approach your handout in two ways: as a sheet of paper to accompany your poster that visitors can take with them, or as a QR code on your poster.

The QR code works really well if it's big, clear and accompanied by 'More info'. Never simply put a QR code on your poster without any explanation. Does the QR code link to a video? Then add 'Watch the video of experiment X'. If it links to a paper, then add 'Download the paper'.

Ideally, the QR code will send your audience to a stand-alone web page on your project website that you created specifically for the poster presentation, or to a PDF on an online platform. That page could include:

1   Your name and contact info (they'll also be on your poster, but include them here too)
2   The abstract
3   A link to your full paper if there is one, or a link to the project website, for example.
4   The references (then you don't have to put them on your poster. Excellent news!)
5   Any extras you want to share (a video, graph, table, more in-depth explanation, etc.)

What also works well is a print-out of your poster on one side of the sheet and the handout on the back. This way, anyone who's interested gets everything in one nice compact format.

Key insight

*Use a handout to remove info
from your poster.*

———

Exercise

Think about what you can put in your handout instead of on your poster. What only makes sense for people who want to dig a lot deeper?

Creating a QR code

Creating a QR code is simple. Type 'QR code generator' into a search engine and you'll get plenty of results. We use QRCode Monkey (qrcode-monkey.com), which even lets you add logos, colours and other extras. There are other services that are just as good, but check the time the QR code stays valid. You don't want to risk creating a QR code that no longer works on the day of the conference.

Summary so far

Your poster is starting to take shape.

1 You identified your audience and made sure your message is tailored to them.

2 You settled on a key message that you repeat in as many places as possible.

3 You wrote a problem–solution–advantage pitch that you'll use for your verbal intro but also in the introduction block of your poster.

4 You created a pyramid structure.

5 You wrote a text of no more than 400 words.

6 You made a handout for the info that won't fit on your poster.

What if your supervisor doesn't agree with our suggestions?

You might already be excited to get started on your poster – we certainly hope so. But you may also be having doubts. We often find that researchers are completely on board with the ideas but are still worried about what their supervisor will say. The posters we propose do look a little different from the standard run-of-the-mill posters. It's true. But that's precisely the point, because we want a poster that both looks good *and* works.

If you're still worried about your supervisor's reaction, consider these points:

1 **It's about impact.** The common approach has little impact. We've been presenting scientific posters in the same way since the 1970s. Every time we show up with reams of text and miss out on a lot of valuable conversations and opportunities. After 50 years, isn't it time to realise that the initial poster experiment doesn't deliver the results we're after and that we need to make a few tweaks? That's exactly what we're proposing: a poster can have real impact, but you have to change a few things to make it better. That may seem daunting, but I'll bet you'll get more more results than with your previous posters.

2 **See it as an experiment.** A poster session is a very safe place to try something new. There's no judging and, unlike a presentation where dozens of people are staring at you, a poster fair is also a less stressful environment.

3 **Relax and enjoy.** What's the worst thing that could happen if you do things a little differently? That not many people would speak to you? That's going to happen anyway if your poster looks like all the other posters at the conference. By doing things differently, you only stand to gain.
Also, whether your research is good or not is determined long before you make your poster. So your poster doesn't make your experiments or data suddenly better or worse. Relax and enjoy the process.

4 **We're here for you.** Is your supervisor (or are you) still not convinced? Then pass on our contact info (info@thefloorisyours.be). We're happy to discuss any doubts you or they may have.

PART 2
Attention

Part 2 **Table of contents**

After the first part of this book, you'll have the contents of your poster nailed down. You've written all the text and come up with a structure, but as you may have noticed, the poster still feels empty and a little bland. It's now time to bring your poster to life by making it more attractive so that it grabs your audience's attention.

Attention isn't a bad thing

Researchers are sometimes afraid to attract attention. They feel that research isn't something you should have to 'sell'. It should speak for itself and not need any bells or whistles. Or they worry that using an eye-catching title or images to attract attention will put their scientific integrity at risk.

But it's essential to include things that attract attention. Remember what we said in the intro, that people read a poster as follows:

1 **Something grabs their attention.** During their tour of the poster session, something makes them stop and look at your poster.

2 **They show interest.** They scan the poster, read the headers and view your poster from a safe distance.

3 **They get excited.** They read the whole poster and start talking to you.

And as we said before: the winning poster is the one that starts the most conversations, not the one that conveys the most information. Attracting attention is an essential part of this. Try strolling past your own poster and see what grabs your attention. Is it the image? The text? The graph? The title? Or nothing at all? Because if there's nothing on your poster that grabs people's attention, they'll simply walk on by.

Should you present your research as more sensational than it really is just to get people's attention? No, definitely not. For example, don't say that your research has found a cure for cancer, because it hasn't. But perhaps your research offers a surprising or interesting way to treat cancer or increase the survival rates of a specific type of cancer. That's sensational enough.

Besides the fear of sensation, there are two other reasons that it's sometimes difficult for researchers to grab people's attention.

1. They often don't see how special their research is.

You may have been working day and night on a subject and no longer think it's particularly special, but for many of us it's the first time we're hearing about it. Example: I've been giving workshops for years at an organisation that has a research laboratory

2 Attention

225 metres underground. It took me seven years to find this out because no researcher thought it was worth mentioning.

In your research, too, there are some fascinating things that you no doubt find pretty standard. Usually these are the things you do every day. Maybe you shoot frozen ducks into aeroplane engines to test their safety, develop ink to 3D-print organs, or for your last experiment had to number five hundred Petri dishes. There are things in your research that will attract attention. You just have to be able to recognise them.

2. They worry that the nuances will be lost.

You will always have to choose something to bring to the fore and then decide what you're going to drop. That's okay. **Be exact, not exhaustive.** You'll never be able to cover everything in a pitch or on a poster. You simply don't have the space or time.

Don't be afraid to draw people's attention to what you've selected as the most relevant information for this audience. Make sure they get enough relevant information to understand your key message, but no more. People who want to hear the full story will come and talk to you, take your handout or read your paper.

Key takeaway

Be exact, not exhaustive. Give people just enough relevant info to understand your key message.

———

Your poster is a teaser

Throughout your poster presentation you're teasing the audience in the hope that you can keep them interested in your story. Your poster is just one part of that.

You can look at it as a funnel that you're trying to draw your audience into as far as possible.

→ **The title and image** on your poster act as a teaser so that you can deliver your **pitch** and encourage your audience to come a bit closer.

→ **Your pitch** acts as a teaser to show them more of your **poster** and start a **conversation**.

→ **Your poster and conversation** also act as a teaser to get them to dig deeper and even read your paper or get in touch.

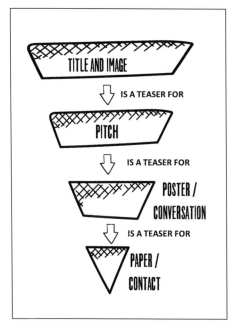

With a good attention grabber, you'll draw more people into your funnel, leading to more conversations and contacts. Without a good attention grabber, you'll start with just a fraction of the people who are potentially interested.

If you put up hurdles along the way, like a difficult title, a chaotic pitch or an unattractive poster crammed full of text, then you lose more and more people at every step, until you're left wondering why nobody wants to talk to you.

As a researcher, it is your job to remove those hurdles. Of course, it all depends on your goal. Perhaps you just want to have two really good conversations with the other subject matter experts at the conference. That's fine. As long as you realise that you'll be missing out on a lot of potentially interesting contacts.

Step 7: Sketch your poster

Thanks to all the work you've done so far, you're almost ready to turn on your computer and start shaping your poster. But hold on just a little longer. First make a sketch of your poster. This *can* be done on a computer, but it's often a lot easier and more intuitive to use pen and paper. While you're sketching, you'll decide roughly where everything will go on your poster.

First an example, then some general tips:

This researcher's sketch puts him well on his way to a good poster. Even as an outsider you can tell what the plan is and that it's heading in the right direction:

→   The researcher is using a clear title (In-vessel Retention of Nuclear Explosion) and a more scientific subtitle (Investigation of Hypothetical Core Disruptive Accident in MYRRHA).
→   He's put the introduction block at the top and in the middle. He wants to put it in a box that includes his key message and

opening sentence (But, Therefore, So that). Ideally, that box will also have a coloured background.

→ He's split the poster up into three columns.

→ In the left-hand column he's going to include a process or flow diagram.

→ Finally, something jumps out at us in the bottom right-hand corner: a number combined with a word and an icon. This is what we like to call a 'font-focused chart' and something we'll come back to in step 11 (page 126) when we talk about data visualisation. All you need to know for now is that a font-focused chart is ideal for conveying a specific number.

2 Attention

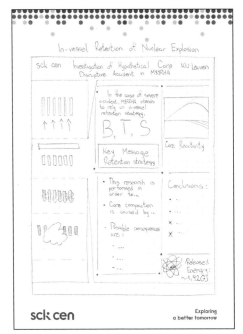

A quick sketch will make your life a lot easier and give you an idea of how your poster will look. It will also save you hours of fiddling around in your design tool. (Sketch by Petrović Đorđe)

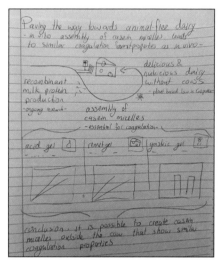

Another example of a simple sketch next to the final version of the poster. Here, too, the researcher opts for a short, clear title and a more scientific subtitle. She also plans to draw a kind of path or process at the top and to elaborate on the second step in three different blocks. Lastly, the conclusion is given a prominent place at the bottom.

Making an initial sketch is a real time-saver. A lot of researchers start their poster by opening up PowerPoint and throwing in all the text they can think of. Then they have to drag, delete and cram it all in. This approach is rarely successful, extremely frustrating and very time-consuming. It's much easier and faster to make changes on a rough sketch than in a cluttered PowerPoint slide.

So pull out a piece of paper and sketch your poster based on your pyramid structure. Once you have done that, you're ready for the next step.

You don't always have to use blocks

Scientific posters are often made up of blocks but I use the word 'block' mainly for convenience's sake. You *can* create a poster with blocks, but you don't have to. You're completely free to try out different designs.

Paving the way towards animal-free dairy
Coagulation behaviour of reassembled and native bovine casein micelles

Renske Bouma, Kasper Hettinga, Etske Bijl, Abigail Thiel

Recombinant milk protein production

On the road to animal-free dairy

Production of animal-free dairy

In milk caseins are present as micelles. Recombinant casein will have to be shaped into micelles to be able to mimic certain products.

Coagulation is only part of the story. Dairy products like cheese need further processing. This will be studied in the future.

Assembly & coagulation of casein micelles

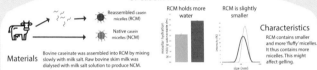

Reassembled casein micelles (RCM)

Native casein micelles (NCM)

Materials Bovine caseinate was assembled into RCM by mixing slowly with milk salt. Raw bovine skim milk was dialysed with milk salt solution to produce NCM.

RCM holds more water

RCM is slightly smaller

Characteristics RCM contains smaller and more 'fluffy' micelles. It thus contains more micelles. This might affect gelling.

Acid gelation

Yoghurt gets its texture from acid gelation. Gelling was induced by GDL which creates a gradual pH drop. Firmness was measured by SOAS as storage modulus increase.

RCM gels at slightly lower pH and forms a weaker acid gel

Renneting

Cheese curd is renneted with the enzyme chymosin. The curd firmness affects process efficiency and cheese quality. Gelling was induced by recombinant chymosin. Firmness was measured by SOAS as storage modulus increase.

RCM rennets faster and forms a firmer curd

Gastric clotting

In the stomach, acid and enzyme cause milk to clot. The gastric clotting affects the rate of nutrition release to the body. Gelling was induced by gradual addition of simulated gastric fluid containing HCl and pepsin. Firmness was assessed by the moisture content of the clot.

RCM forms a slightly drier gastric clot

This publication is part of the 'Animal-free milk proteins' project (with project number NWA.1292.19.302) of the NWA research programme 'Research along Routes by Consortia (ORCY', which is funded by the Dutch Research Council (NWO).

WAGENINGEN UNIVERSITY & RESEARCH

Contact the presenter: renske.bouma@wur.nl or connect on LinkedIn

Conclusion & future outlook

- Reassembled casein micelles coagulate in relevant conditions
- Coagulation behaviour does differ with native casein micelles
- This knowledge will be used to assemble recombinant protein and to guide the development of animal-free dairy.

An initial sketch (left) and the final poster, where you can clearly see the path and the three blocks. By sketching her poster first, the researcher came up with original ideas that she probably wouldn't have had if she'd jumped straight into using a design tool (poster by Renske Bouma).

Below you'll find some examples of poster designs that don't use the standard blocks. Let your creativity run wild! Need more inspiration? Then search on Pinterest using terms like 'research poster template'. You often get better results on Pinterest than Google Images and you can quickly save them in a handy list to look at in more detail later on. By looking at different research posters, you will quickly see which ones you like and which ones you don't. In this phase, focus on how they are built.

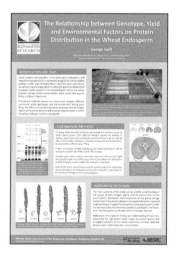

◄ A poster with a classic block design. But you don't always have to use blocks (poster by George Savill).

▼ 1. Three columns, but with a small twist: the columns are curved. Small tweaks to a standard design immediately grab people's attention.

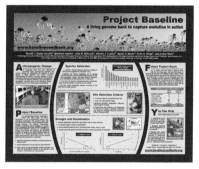

1. One, two, three or four columns

This example has three columns, with the added twist that the columns are not straight but curved. This makes it stand out straight away.

Numerical Modelling of Binary Collision of Adhesive Units

Sohan Sarangi[1], Kyrre Thalberg[2], Göran Alderborn[1], Göran Frenning[1]

1. Department of Pharmacy, Uppsala University, Uppsala, Sweden
2. Inhalation Product Development, Pharmaceutical Technology & Development, Astra Zeneca, Gothenburg, Sweden

1 Introduction

Drug delivery through dry powder inhalers (DPI) is becoming a popular means of treating pulmonary and respiratory diseases. DPIs use micronized active pharmaceutical ingredient (API) (< 5μm) to reach the deep lungs.

This study focuses on binary collisions between adhesive units with low impact velocity mimicking the handling situation.

Setup

Binary head on collisions between adhesive units was studied with a focus on stability ratios (stay ratio, transfer ratio, loss ratio) and restitution coefficient (the ratio between the average relative velocity of carriers after and before collision). Different surface energy and Surface Coverage Ratio (SCR) was considered and a total of 540 independent

2 Methods

The computational tool used in this study is the Discrete Element Method (DEM) for simulation of binary collisions of monodispersed adhesive units. DEM uses Newton's second law of motion to calculate forces between particle. Particles are modelled as elastic non-deformable sphere. Van der Waals force is the most significant force that governs interactions between adhesive units, which is represented as a surface energy between particles. Surface energy resulting in cohesive force between API-API and carrier-API were represented by JKR adhesion theory.

SCR 0.5 SCR 0.7 SCR 1

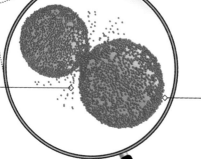

Adhesive Unit

APIs and carrier particles were modelled as elastic spheres of 3μm and 100μm aerodynamic diameter, respectively. Adhesive units were formed by pseudo randomized distribution of API particles on the surface of the carrier. Different number density of API on carrier surface is considered defined by surface coverage ratio (SCR).

3 Results

4 Conclusion

Dynamics of adhesive unit is complex and difficult to represent by a simple mathematical equation of carrier and API properties. A detailed analysis of binary collisions was performed and stable regimes for handling inhalable dry powder were determined. The obtained results provide a step forward of the understanding of the mechanics of adhesive units and can be used to improve the flowability and handling of micronized dry powders.

References
[1] R. Arjan and S. Chathi, "Dry powder inhalers: DiPha-A review of device reliability and innovation," Int. J. Pharm., vol. 360, no. 1–2, pp. 1–11, 2016.
[2] K. Johnson, K. Kendall, and A. D. Roberts, "Surface Energy and the Contact of Elastic Solids," Proc. R. Soc. A Math. Phys. Eng. Sci., vol. 324, no. 1558, pp. 310–313, 1971.
[3] D. Nguyen, A. Rasmuson, K. Thalberg, and I. Niklasson Björn, "Numerical modelling of breakage and adhesion of loose fine-particle agglomerates," Chem. Eng. Sci., vol. 116, pp. 91–98, 2014.

This study is part of the science program of the Swedish Drug Delivery Forum (SDDF)

sohan.sarangi@farmaci.uu.se

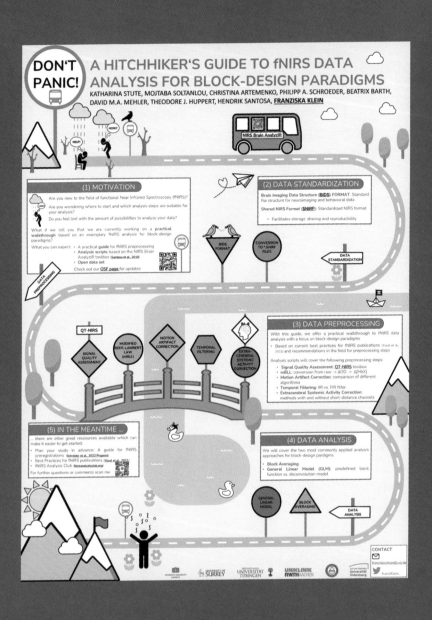

A path is an ideal way to illustrate a step-by-step approach (poster by Franziska Klein).

2. A circle in the middle

Place a message or image in a circle in the middle and the rest of your text around it.

3. A path

Ideal for illustrating a process. Doesn't necessarily have to be as nicely presented as this example. It could also be just a simple line with bubbles coming out of it or with simple icons.

4. A large image

A large central image is a great attention grabber. You could use a photo, icon or illustration. Illustrations stand out particularly well because they're not very common on posters.

5. A background that fills the entire poster

Look for a big photo to fill the entire background of your poster. Choose a background that has enough space and that contrasts with your text. Make the image more transparent if it's difficult to read the poster text. We'll go into more detail about images on page 102.

The examples in this section illustrate just a few of the potential ideas. So sketch away and come up several different iterations.

Exercise
Take a piece of paper and create a sketch. It's often much easier to do this on paper than on a computer.

2 Attention

Large images really attract the attention (poster by Mollie Slater-Baker and Erinn Fagan-Jeffries).

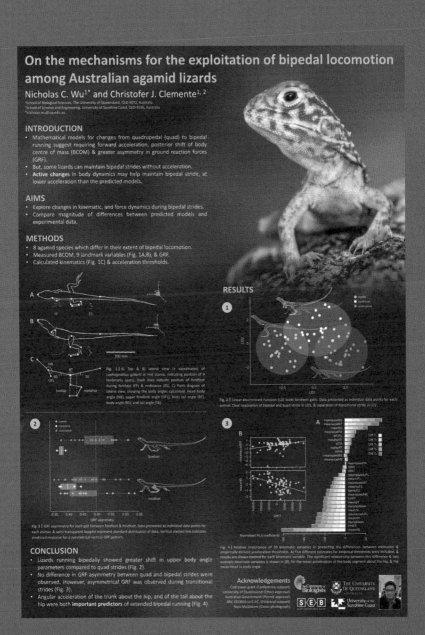

Images that fill the whole of the poster can look really nice. Make sure you stick to the same colour scheme used in the image (poster by Nicholas Wu).

Interlude

Ignore your institution's template (or at least some of it)

At this point you might be thinking, 'I see the advantage of this approach to scientific posters, but unfortunately I've got a template I have to stick to.' If your organisation or the conference you're attending has given you a template to use, I hereby give you permission to ignore most of said template. Don't panic. I'll explain in a moment what you can ignore and why.

Templates often look like this:

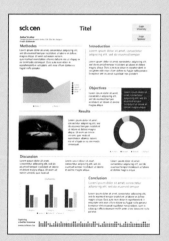

A template often simply adopts the same structure as a paper. Ignore it if you want to.

There is a designated block for introduction, method, results, discussion and conclusions. In other words, organisations simply adopt the same structure found in papers or on other posters without putting a lot of thought into it. As we mentioned earlier, this structure is one way to design a poster but certainly not the best.

And the communications team that develops the poster template doesn't usually take this into account. The only thing you really need to use from a template is this:

Use only the header and footer of a template.
And do whatever you want with the rest. To improve this empty template even further, we'd move the logos to the bottom to allow more space for the title (poster and template by SCK CEN).

As long as you don't touch the header and footer, most people are happy. But why does a communications team create a template then? So that the posters from their institution look roughly the same and external parties can clearly see which organisation you belong to. By keeping the header (often with logos) and the footer (often with contact details and some kind of corporate branding), you achieve the same goal.

But everything in between is a blank canvas where you can do whatever you want. Go ahead and create your own structure or design. If you've been given a template, delete the middle section and instead use the tips we've given you. Admittedly, there is comfort in following a template to the letter. You don't have to put any thought into it. You simply fill it in, copy/paste your text and stay under the radar. It's the safe option. The result, however, is that your poster will look the same as all the others: a wall of text that people just walk straight past. No cross-pollination of ideas, no conversations. So step out of that comfort zone, and try something different.

80

PHD essentials

That being said, besides the header and footer, there are two other things you should keep from a template:

1. **The colour scheme:** your institution has specific colours that you'll also find in the template. Use these.
2. **The fonts:** the communications team probably thought long and hard about which fonts fit together nicely and what style they convey. Here too: there is no reason to start looking for other fonts.

But the rest is completely up to you.

Belgian Nuclear Research Centre SCK CEN (whose template we could use here as an example, see the image on the right) recognises this too. Next to the template they make available to their researchers, they say: 'Feel free to change the layout between the Header and Footer. You can use this example as inspiration.' And that says it all: a template serves as inspiration.

What if the conference imposes a template?

Sometimes the conference you're going to will impose a template. Why do they do that? They provide guidelines to avoid problems, like posters that are too large, too small or that have the wrong orientation. And they want the posters to look good.

So when you're reading the guidelines provided by the conference, always follow the spirit rather than the letter of the law. For example, if the guidelines say that you have to mention your method, results and conclusions, this doesn't mean you necessarily have to divide the poster into the standard method–results–conclusions blocks. They are just asking you to talk about your method somewhere.

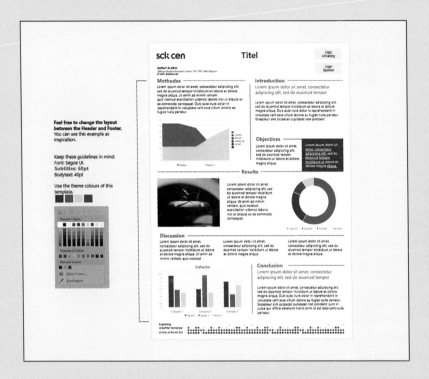

The guidelines on how to deal with a conference template are very similar to how to deal with your institution's template: keep the header, footer, colours and fonts, but otherwise do your own thing. Be sure to check and stick to the required dimensions and orientation. You don't want to show up with a landscape poster to find that they only have portrait poster panels at the conference.

2 Attention

Step 8: Come up with an attention-grabbing title

Your title is a crucial piece of text. It's often the first thing the audience will read, and those few words need to steal their attention away from all the other titles and words at a poster fair. To achieve its goal *and* have impact, a title should be quick to read and understand.

Researchers often think their poster title needs to match the full title of their paper or PhD. But that's not true. Paper or PhD titles are often complex and take some time to understand. Time your audience simply doesn't have at a poster fair. In just a few seconds, they want to be able to decide whether they're interested in your topic. That's why your title needs to immediately sell your poster to your visitors.

Above all, remember: a title doesn't must summarise the whole thing, just attract attention. It needs to promise the audience compelling content in exchange for a few minutes of their valuable time. A powerful title is worth its weight in gold, so make sure you put enough thought into it.

Make sure people understand your title without having to read the whole poster first

It is precisely because a title is an important entry point for your poster that people should be able to understand it without having to read the rest of the poster first. So don't use words in your title that your audience has never heard of. The only exception to this is if you decide to use jargon in your title to attract a specific type of audience. Only want to talk to people who know what SEM (Scanning Electron Microscopy) is? Then put it in your title, but be aware that you won't attract anyone who's never heard of SEM. So perhaps a better header for this section would be: Make sure *the people you want to reach* understand your title without having to read the whole poster first.

This links back to what we said earlier: avoid abbreviations and acronyms in titles. A project name like SCATMAN (Stroke CAvities Treatment Mechanism with Active Neural interfaces) might be amusing but it won't mean anything to your audience. So it doesn't belong in your poster title.

Make your title your key message

This isn't a must-have but definitely worth considering because you've already written out your key message in one sentence without any jargon. This makes it the ideal candidate for your title and usually a much better option than the title of your research.

Keep your title short

Short titles are by far the best option. Easier said than done, because a lot of research titles are a tangled web of subordinate clauses and colons. How long is too long for a title? If you use a font size of 96 points for your title and it fits on a maximum of two lines, then it's fine. If your title starts taking up three or four lines, you need to shorten it.

Is your title short enough for you to make it even bigger than 96 points? Then go for it. You can even go up to 120 points. Any bigger than that will be extremely big and then it depends a bit on the design of the rest of the poster.

Short titles simply work better. Look at the examples on the next page of a long and short title for the same research. Which poster would you want to read?

→ **Title that's too long:** Repositioning Higher Education as a Global Commodity: Opportunities and challenges for future sociology of education work
→ **Shorter, better title:** The impact of governance and funding on higher education

As another example, look at the short title in the following pitch poster. A poster that the researcher came up with in less than an hour during a workshop.

The title 'Real Men Eat Meat' is short, easy to remember and clearly explains what the research is about. If you want to know more, there is the subtitle and, of course, the rest of the poster.

REAL MEN EAT MEAT

Qualitative Research on the Cultural Construction of Masculinities in Relation to (Red) Meat Consumption

Did you know that masculinity and eating meat are historically and culturally linked to each other? And that the saying 'real men eat meat' permeates our culture?

PROBLEM

Mostly Men consume meat in higher quantities and this consumption of meat translates into gender differences in health problems which are related to an overconsumption of meat.

SOLUTION

The research focuses on the cultural construction of Western masculinities in relation to meat comsuption, so that we gain insight in the underlying cultural process that may contribute to men's increased meat consumption that concerns associations between eating meat and beliefs about masculinities.

RELEVANCE

We aim a better understanding of the connections between eating meat and beliefs about masculinity, which may play an important role in achieving health and sustainability objectives.

For more info and contact details

 Universiteit Antwerpen   UNIVERSITEIT GENT   fwo

Short titles have more impact (poster by Elina Vrijsen).

Add a subtitle

You can provide more information in a subtitle. Like in the 'Real Men Eat Meat' example, where the subtitle reads: 'Quantitative research on the Cultural Construction of Masculinities in relation to (Red) meat consumption.'

The subtitle is often a good place to provide details like the method you used or the exact organism you studied. If your key message isn't in the title itself, then the subtitle is the best place to put it.

THE IDIOPATHIC EPILEPSY MYSTERY

Plasma and faecal metabolome are different in dogs with idiopathic epilepsy

F. Verdoodt[1,2,3] ✉ Fien.Verdoodt@Ugent.be, L.Y. Hemeryck[2], L.Vanhaecke[2], L. Van Ham[3], M. Hesta[1], S.F.M. Bhatti[3]

[1]Equine and Companion Animal Nutrition, [2]Laboratory of Integrative Metabolomics, [3]Small Animal Department - Faculty of Veterinary Medicine, Ghent University, Merelbeke, Belgium

A short, attention-grabbing title with the key message in the subtitle.

If your title is too long, see if you can split it in two and move part of it to the subtitle. For example, do you have a colon in your title? This often indicates the point where an independent clause is introduced, the ideal place to split the title in two. The part before the colon then becomes the title and the part after the colon the subtitle.

By splitting your title into a title and a subtitle, you make sure that the key information stands out. And an added benefit: if your supervisor isn't keen on your entertaining title, you can keep them happy with a more technical subtitle.

Using green solvents in restoration: application of biomass-derived solvents in cleaning procedures

USING GREEN SOLVENTS IN RESTORATION
Application of biomass-derived solvents in cleaning procedures

Tip: split a title at a colon. Make one part the title and the other the subtitle.

Laser cleaning of paint layers on white marble surface based on cooperative use of laser-induced breakdown spectroscopy and image binarization

LASER CLEANING OF PAINT LAYERS ON WHITE MARBLE
based on cooperative use of laser-induced
breakdown spectroscopy and image binarization

Tip: put details like the method used in the subtitle.

You're allowed to change your title

Perhaps you had to submit a title six months before the conference so that the organisers could make their selection for the poster fair. If while you're creating your poster you come up with a better or more accurate title, that's okay. It's very difficult to say exactly what your poster will look like six months in advance. Titles are notoriously difficult to write and people rarely get it right the first time. Do you feel the need to put a different title on your poster than the one you already submitted? Then do it.

Some tips for a good title

1. Use numbers
A number in the title sparks interest and provides structure. Example: Five myths about organic food.

2. Ask a question or make a statement
Challenge your audience. Asking a question or making a statement gets them thinking. Statements are often more effective than questions.
Original title: Entomofagy: an innovative nutritional navigational tool in the race for food security.
As a question: Can we feed the world by eating insects?
As a statement: We can feed the world by eating insects.

3. Make surprising connections
Link your research or project to everyday life. Or bring together two things that at first glance have nothing to do with each other. Example: Limburg cheese cures malaria.

4. Choose popular words
As researchers or professionals, we prefer to keep our distance from trends. But certain words simply attract more attention than others. Example: Cells have sex too.

5. Use verbs

A verb makes your title more active and less vague. Example:

→ Without verb: The relationship between young professionals & their seniors

→ With verb: Why young professionals **shouldn't** always **imitate** their seniors

Interlude
Make a pitch poster

You now have a better idea of how to create an expert poster. But to be honest, even if you get it right, there are a lot of events where an expert poster doesn't work at all.

For example, as a researcher you often attend events where the audience isn't an expert in your domain. You certainly deserve the materials-expert spot at that climate conference, but don't expect the biologist, food technologist, economist or psychologist who are also there to understand or want to read your expert poster about perovskite structures.

An expert poster doesn't work so well at certain events, from interdisciplinary conferences and industry meetings to online presentations and study days. That's why, in addition to the expert poster, we propose a second poster format: the pitch poster. A pitch poster is exactly as described: your pitch on a poster. You may not be familiar with this approach yet, so let's change that now.

What does a pitch poster look like?

For a pitch poster, you take the elements of your introductory pitch and put them on a poster. They're quick and easy to make and work better than the typical scientific posters at a lot of events. Let's first look at how to put together a pitch poster and then go into more detail about where you can use it.

The original pitch we want to use for our pitch poster is about how we can turn food-industry waste into useful substances and looks like this:

> The food industry generates a lot of waste, like residues of wine-making or peels from the juice industry.
>
> BUT these wastes contain valuable compounds that we don't use right now, compounds that could be used in chemical industry and agriculture.
>
> THEREFORE we aim to develop biotechnical processes like enzymatic synthesis or fermentation that use food waste as a starting point to obtain a variety of compounds which for example can be used on fields to protect crops.
>
> SO THAT we can use these food residues as raw materials to obtain high value chemicals in a more environmentally friendly way. These chemicals can in turn protect crops.

The pitch poster then looks like this:

2 Attention

REUSE ORANGE PEEL TO PROTECT CROPS
Extracting valuable compounds out of food waste

Orange peel look like waste, but is actually very valuable. Peel contains interesting compounds like fibers or oils. With this research we want to develop the technology to extract these materials and reuse the waste.

Want to know more? Talk to me or scan the QR code.

CONTACT
toon@thefloorisyours.be

Still useful to make compounds that can protect crops!

Valuable compounds are thrown away

The food industry generates a lot of waste, like **residues from winemaking or peel from the juice industry**. This waste contains **valuable compounds that we don't use right now**, but that can be used in chemical industry and agriculture.

Synthesis & fermentation

We aim to develop **biotechnical processes, like enzymatic sythesis or fermentation,** that use food waste as a starting point to obtain a variety of compounds. These can then be used for example in fields to protect crops.

High-value chemicals

We can use food residue as raw materials to **obtain high-value chemicals in a more environmentally friendly way.** These chemicals can in turn protect crops.

A pitch poster is a useful poster format for occasions where an expert poster doesn't work.

The five elements of a pitch poster:

1 **A short attention-grabbing title,** possibly supplemented with a more technical subtitle. The title needs to grab the audience's attention, but also quickly clarify what the poster is about. If possible, also include your key message in your title. We talked about titles in step 8 (page 82).

2 **A clear key message** that is given a lot of space. We already talked about the importance of a clear key message in step 2 (page 30). On a pitch poster you can expand that key message to around three sentences.

3 **Three blocks.** A block each for the problem, solution and advantage. In those three blocks you explain (1) the challenge that you're researching, (2) the solution you want to provide with your research and (3) the advantage of the research for your audience. You get these elements from the introductory pitch you prepared in step 3 (page 40). We also recommend replacing the words 'problem', 'solution' and 'advantage' with more descriptive titles, like in the example on the left-hand page.

4 **A large image.** Images grab people's attention and make them stop at your poster. An image makes it immediately clear what your research is about. In step 9 (page 102) we'll go into more detail about where to find good images.

5 **A QR code and contact info.** A QR code can be used to provide a lot of extra info. Like an abstract, references, extra graphs, a handout, link to your latest publication or project website, or any other information that doesn't fit on your pitch poster. We talked about handouts and QR codes in step 6 (page 57).

These are the five elements of a pitch poster. Resist the temptation to add more. A pitch poster clocks in at around 150–200 words. Anyone who wants to know more will come and speak to you or

2 Attention

scan the QR code. And before you know it, you'll be having a real conversation.

Often a better choice than a typical scientific poster

As you've maybe never seen one before, you might think that a pitch poster isn't appropriate for scientific events, but in fact the opposite is true. There are many situations where a pitch poster works much better than a typical scientific poster. For example:

Your poster is being projected

→ Imagine for a moment that you've been asked to give **a shotgun presentation**. This is where you're invited onto the stage to give a three-minute presentation while your poster is projected behind you. You're then followed by ten other researchers all doing the same thing.

The challenge with a shotgun presentation is that a projector has a much lower resolution than a printed sheet of paper. Text or graphics that look fine when printed out are almost unreadable when they're projected. Your audience is then left with just your images and titles that are easy to read. If you want to make your text and graphs readable too, you need to make everything a lot bigger.

What's the best way to approach a shotgun presentation then? You definitely don't want to be standing with your back to your audience the whole time, pointing out the unreadable things on your poster. Treat your act more like a presentation than a normal poster session. Show things, ask questions, and use hand gestures and facial expressions to get your point across effectively. Your audience will mainly want to use your poster as a visual aid. With a pitch poster you achieve all these things: the poster has enough info and provides the right level of support for you to successfully complete your short pitch.

You're attending a research day

→ A typical research day at an institution brings together researchers from different disciplines or faculties. You then have to explain your research about, say, a protein in the blood to a researcher who works in machine learning. Or vice versa. It doesn't help anyone if you show up with your extremely detailed, text-heavy poster. A pitch poster is the way to go.

You're at a focus day or online poster presentation

→ If you're presenting your poster during a focus day for researchers as well as policy makers and patients, for example, a standard scientific poster isn't helpful. It's too detailed and too difficult. A pitch poster works much better.
A pitch poster is also the ideal approach for online presentations, interdisciplinary conferences, poster sessions for companies, etc.

In short: Whenever it might be difficult to read your poster or you have an audience that isn't full of experts, you're best off choosing a pitch poster instead of a more standard expert poster. And best of all? Making a pitch poster is quick and easy to do. All you need is the pitch you wrote earlier.

Long live the pitch poster!

Award-winning pitch posters in South Africa

Hans, one of the authors of this book, was invited to a conference in South Africa where they organised shotgun-poster presentations. Before the event, we gave the researchers poster training, during which they learnt how to make a pitch poster. Some applied the tips to their poster, while others stuck to the traditional scientific poster. At the end of the poster session, there was an awards ceremony for the best poster presentations. And guess what? The top three winners all used a pitch poster (and no, we weren't on the jury). Later, researcher Nicolle Claasen used the same pitch poster for a five-minute poster presentation at another conference and she won again.

Some more pitch poster examples

Looking for more inspiration? Lots of researchers have made pitch posters about their research. On the following pages are some examples of posters that have been used at conferences and posters that were made after a workshop.

Are your food containers as safe as your food?

Beyond the scoop: investigating potential allergen risks when buying food in bulk

Shopping in bulk has emerged as a conscious and eco-friendly approach to food procurement. However, this trend raises important questions about the containers used for food transportation and storage, access to allergen-related information, and the risk of cross-contamination.

Take the survey and help us find the answer!

1,2 billion € by 2030
Mid-estimate EU market for bulk goods

~ 11-26 million
members of the European population suffering from food allergies

Methodology

1	3	3	5	38
Online Survey LimeSurvey software	**Regions** Flanders, Brussels, Wallonia	**Languages** Dutch, English, French	**Themes** User profiling, Motivation, Consumer data on purchasing and storage, Allergen information availability, COVID-19 pandemic influence	**Questions** Discussed with stakeholders

The research that yielded these results was funded by the Belgian Federal Public Service of Health, Food Chain Safety and Environment through the contract TREFCOM (RT 21/4).

Do you want to know more? Get in touch!

Sciensano · Salvatore Ciano · T + 32 2 642 54 29 · **.be**
salvatore.ciano@sciensano.be · **www.sciensano.be**

Salvatore Ciano used this pitch poster to clearly convey his key message: 'Take the survey.'

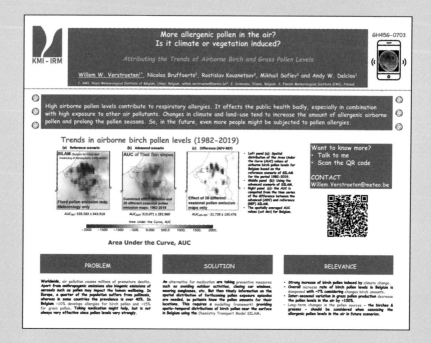

Willem Verstraeten made this pitch poster for a climate conference with an impressive 25,000 attendees. Every day there were 2,500 new posters to look at. It was almost an impossible task for him to make his work stand out from the crowd and to strike up conversations. But he told us he wasn't once bored during his three-hour poster session, something he'd not experienced with previous posters he made. Another benefit, according to him: it was also quicker to make.

Place names tell the history of the landscape (or not?)

Place names **often refer to** historical landscape features
But the **link between place name and landscape stays** obscure
Can we unravel **this link by using** data driven methods?
And are these techniques useful for wetland reconstruction?

Can we make a machine learning model that predicts wetland presence based on place name data?

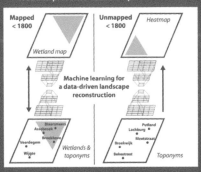

16th century

18th century

19th century

Problem

Knowledge on continuity and change between place names and the landscape remains obscure...

When and under which *circumstances* do toponyms change in meaning and space?

Solution

Digital methods such as GIS and machine learning will be applied to analyse toponymic data and landscape features extracted from historical maps (16th-20th century).

Relevance

Insight into how place names are related to the landscape enables to reconstruct wetlands. These insights can be used for present wetland restoration projects.

Want to know more?
Visit the project website!

 Christophe De Coster
Christophe.decoster@uantwerpen.be

A pitch poster about the link between place names and history. What works well here is the red and yellow colour scheme. The QR code also grabs the audience's attention. Putting part of the title in a different colour is also a nice touch (poster by Christophe De Coster).

Biomarkers for obsessive-compulsive disorder (OCD)

A new approach to objectively quantify and monitor OCD symptom severity throughout cognitive behavioural therapy (CBT) and deep brain stimulation (DBS)

Xena Serifova, Stephanie Van der Donck, Laura Luyten, Hannes Heylen, Myles Mc Laughlin, Chris Bervoets & Bart Boets - KU Leuven, Belgium

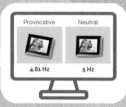
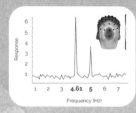
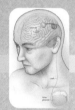

PROBLEM

There is **no objective biomarker** to determine the severity of OCD-related symptoms, which complicates treatment choice and evaluation.

SOLUTION

We combine **symptom provocation** with neural, behavioural, and physical responses to objectively quantify OCD-related symptomatology. We assess **neural saliency** (frequency-tagging EEG and low-frequency oscillation power), **attentional orienting** (eye tracking) and **stress physiology** (heart rate and skin conductance).

RELEVANCE

We apply these methods to monitor change throughout **CBT** and **DBS** interventions. This multimodal integrative approach may significantly enhance our understanding of OCD-related symptomatology and thereby contribute to the development of a reliable neurophysiological **biomarker for OCD**.

Scan this QR-code for more information

CONTACT
xena.serifova@kuleuven.be

Pitch poster by Xena Serifova.

What works well here is its short, punchy title, attention-grabbing image and consistent use of the colour green.

A pitch poster about the link between eating meat and culture, by Elina Vrijsen.

On the left hand page a really nice pitch poster about research on Obsessive Compulsive Disorder (OCD). Xena Serifova wasn't sure whether this poster would also be appropriate for a conference. But it certainly is. The poster will act as a great conversation starter, although I would perhaps take along some printed-out data like tables or graphs so I could share these if someone wants to dig deeper or if I want to support certain statements with data. Later, Xena informed us that "people were ready to speak to me before I had fully set the poster up. I spoke with several researchers and also made arrangements to discuss our findings together in the future when I have more results. I also received a promising proposal for possible collaboration."

We hope these pitch posters make you want to give it a try for your own research. Another tip: it's not really in the scope of this book, but a pitch poster isn't that far off the graphic abstract a lot of conferences ask for these days. You will still need to adjust the format and the info, but it's an excellent starting point.

Step 9: Find the perfect image

Images are powerful because they grab people's attention. Walk around a conference centre full of posters, and it's the ones with a big image that are bound to catch your eye. They also immediately tell you what it's about. For example, look at the following poster title:

Unraveling uranium uptake mechanisms in Arabidopsis thaliana

From the title alone, it might be clear that it's about the absorption of uranium, but you probably won't get much further than that. What if the researcher adds the image below? Now you know straight away what it's about: a plant that absorbs uranium.

An image immediately makes it clear what the research is about.

An image is a big help when it comes to conveying information, especially if visitors only have a few seconds to decide whether they're interested in your poster. By combining an image with text, you appeal to both the textual and visual brain of your audience, and they retain the information much better.

Where to find images?

The list of websites where you can find good-quality images is constantly changing and improving. But the rule of thumb is: use Google Images only after you've exhausted all other options. That's because with Google Images you often run into issues with copyright (not everything on Google can simply be used) and resolution (the resolution of photos on Google is often too low, which means they quickly become blurry on your large poster).

Below you'll find a few good websites for images. Always remember to check whether you need to credit the owner of the image.

Photos

1 **Pexels.com:** high-quality photos, free to use.
2 **Unsplash.com:** similar to pexels.com, but another database.
3 **Office 365:** Office's photo database used to be incredibly bad. But now they have a nice collection of photos, icons and illustrations. Definitely worth giving it another chance.

Illustrations

Illustrations often lend a refreshing, original touch to a poster. Precisely because they're not used a lot.

→ **Biorender.com** and **Smart.servier.com:** On both sites you'll find high-quality illustrations related to life sciences. From organs to cells and from lab materials to proteins. Biorender is the most extensive, and it even lets you compose and create figures yourself. The paid version is relatively pricey, though. Smart.servier is more limited in its functionality but is free and easy to use.

2 Attention

→ **Canva.com:** An online design tool that you can use to design your whole poster, but also to find great ready-made design elements and illustrations. There is a limited free version but also a free trial period for the paid version.

→ **Fiverr.com:** A website where you can pay for freelance services online. Are you looking for some nice images for your project, a great line drawing or a very specific illustration that you're never going to find on the internet? At fiverr.com you can commission a custom illustration. Often very affordable and with great results. For example, we had this lightbulb logo made for the Battle of the Scientists, an event we organise.

→ **Do it yourself:** If you're not particularly artistic, this might seem like too much of a challenge, but a lot of the most attractive posters I've seen feature self-made illustrations, usually hand-drawn and then digitised. You can digitise a drawing and use it on a poster by scanning it and removing the white background or by creating it directly in a digital drawing app like Adobe Fresco. A handmade image is original and immediately stands out. Are you good with a pencil or pen? Then definitely give it a try.

Icons

The big advantage of icons is that you can easily combine them. Put five icons together on a poster, and it looks good. Put five *photos* on a poster, and it quickly starts to look like a real mess. So icons are a quick and easy way to improve the design of your poster. But watch out: using too many icons isn't good either. Avoid turning your poster into a comic book.

→ **Thenounproject.com:** Offering millions of black-and-white icons, this is one of my all-time favourite websites. You can also add colour to the icons if you want. Really useful for putting on your poster, but also on your project website, in presentations, a video, brochure, etc.

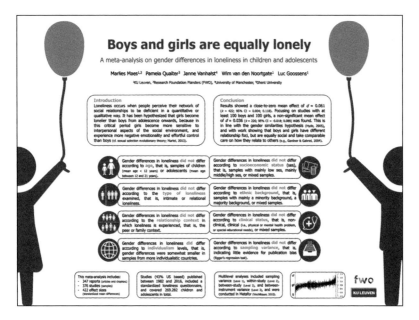

This poster uses a lot of icons, but it all comes together nicely and looks good (poster by Marlies Maes).

→ **Flaticon.com:** A wider range of icon styles than The Noun Project. But that can also be a disadvantage because the different icon styles don't always look good together.

Artificial intelligence

There are lots of artificial-image generators out there that are ideal if you're looking for a photo you can't find on the internet. For example, the image of a baby in a hospital on Zsofia Bognar's poster on the next page, which was a challenge to come up with. She couldn't use any photos of her own patients or find anything on the internet that was quite right. In the photo she wanted not only the child but also the right medical equipment. After a few goes using **Bing Image Creator**, it was **DALL·E 2 from labs.openai.com** that finally generated the following image. And it was exactly what she was looking for. AI is a fun toy with endless possibilities. Be careful you don't waste too much time on it, but it can definitely help you find that perfect image for your poster.

Dries Byloos was looking for a photo of a tall timber-frame building, but these kinds of structures don't exist (yet). So he had a photo created using Bing Image Generator (bottom left of the poster).

sciensano

Can we save more babies?

Group B Streptococcus maternal colonization and neonatal sepsis in Belgium between 2012 and 2021

What is GBS?

- Neonatal Group B Streptococcus (GBS) is one of the leading cause in neonatal infectious morbidity
- Maternal genital GBS colonization can lead to early onset neonatal infection
- GBS vaginal screening of pregnant women between 35-37 gestational week, in case of carriage, intrapartum antibiotic prophylaxis (IAP) is recommended

RESULTS

Maternal screening for GBS, 2012-2021:

- 1,081,001 pregnant women giving live birth recorded (average 120,111 /year)

- 975,950 pregnant women were screened for GBS (average 108,439/year)
- Proportion of pregnant women screened: 90% - stable

- 181,644 pregnant women tested GBS positive (average 20,183/year)
- Of screened, proportion of women tested positive: 19% - stable

Conclusion

- Besides existing preventive guideline still considerable number of neonatal GBS cases could be prevented.

- Proportion of screened pregnant women and administration of intrapartum antibiotic prophylaxis (IAP) require a lot of sources, however still not adhering to guidelines perfectly.

- Rates of maternal colonization and neonatal GBS incidence is comparable to European countries

- Our study provides baseline data for future preventive strategies in GBS prevention such as maternal immunisation

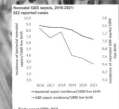

Proportions of pregnant women by their GBS colonization status and by IAP administration

Belgium, 2012-2025

Neonatal GBS sepsis, 2016-2021:
622 reported cases

- bacterial sepsis incidence/1000 live birth
- GBS sepsis incidence/1000 live birth

- Early onset GBS: 81%
- Male : female ratio 1,4 : 1 (P36.0)
- 1-4 fatal cases/year (P36.0)

METHODS

- Calculating proportion of pregnancies where women were GBS-screened, colonized and administered IAP, eBirth certificates, 2012-2020

- Estimating incidence of neonatal all bacterial and GBS sepsis (<1year) in Belgium, hospital diagnosis-based ICD-10 codes, 2016-2021 (P36.8 , A40.1)

Zs.Bognar[1,2] • C. Leroy [3] • V. Van Leeuw [3] < R. Goemaes [4] • P. Melin [5] • C. Meex [5] • R. Sacheli [5] • L.Cornelissen[2]
1. «ECDC Fellowship Programme, Field Epidemiology path (EPIET), European Centre for Disease Prevention and Control (ECDC), Stockholm, Sweden» • 2. «Department of Epidemiology and Public Health, Sciensano» 3. Centre d'Épidémiologie Périnatale (CEpiP), Belgium • 4. Studiecentrum voor Perinatale Epidemiologie (SPE), Belgium • 5. Centre National de Référence (CNR NRC) Streptococcus agalactiae (GBS), CHU Liège, Belgium.

Sciensano • Zsofia Bognar • T + 32 2 642 57 42 • Zsofia.Bognar@sciensano.be • www.sciensano.be

REFERENCES
- Prevention of perinatal Group B Streptococcus infections, Guidelines from the Belgian Health Council, 2003 (SHC.7721)
- Group B streptococcus infection during pregnancy and infancy: estimates of regional and global burden, Gonçalves BP et al. The Lancet Global Health June 2022

.be

Zsofia Bognar couldn't find any photos of children in hospital that she was allowed or wanted to use. So she generated the main photo on this poster using DALL·E 2.

Google Images

As you've just seen, there are plenty of alternatives to find images, but if you do have to turn to Google Images, click on 'Tools' after you've done your search. This gives you more filters, two of which are useful for us:

1 **Size:** always choose 'Large'. A smaller image, no matter how beautiful or suitable it is, will look blurry on your big poster.

2 **Usage Rights:** go for 'Creative Commons licenses'. In short, this indicates that you can use the photos for non-commercial purposes, provided you credit the owner. This means you filter out photos from press agencies or portfolio websites, for example, and you're less likely to find a photo that you're not allowed to use. The chance that someone will fine you for using a photo unlawfully is small, but you wouldn't be the first researcher whose poster goes online only for the press agency to discover it and send you a bill.

Using Google Images? Then filter by Size and Usage Rights.

What images should you look for?

In principle, you can put any image on your poster, as long as the resolution is high enough. But some images are better than others. Try to take note of the following:

Negative space

Do you want an image that fills the whole poster? Then look for one with a lot of negative space. This means that the photo allows plenty of space for text and figures. For example, if you're doing research into aviation, the following photo has barely any negative space. You can only fit a small amount of text on it, making it a bad choice for a poster background.

This next image has a ton of negative space and is pretty much perfect. You could put your title above the plane and your text between the plane and the mountains.

This photo has hardly any negative space, meaning it's not the right choice for your poster's background image.

This is a better image for your poster background because it gives you a lot of space for text or graphic elements.

2 Attention

Transparent background

Putting an image with a transparent background on your poster is easier and makes it more attractive. If the photo has a white background and your poster doesn't, there will be an ugly white box around your image. It's also a lot more difficult to put text on or around that photo.

Logos get a special mention here. Always look for a version of your organisation's logo with a transparent background. There's nothing uglier than a whole load of logos in white boxes on your poster.

Icons or illustrations tend to have a transparent background. When it comes to photos, you'll have to look a little harder, but:

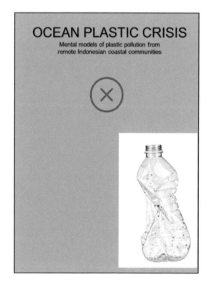
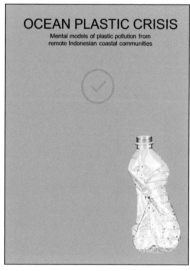

Search for images or logos without a white background. Images with a white background can only be used on a white poster.

→ On pngwing.com you'll find plenty of images without a background.

→ You can use the online photo editor photopea.com to easily make simple edits to photos, like selecting and removing the background.

→ If you're searching on Google Images, put 'Filetype: .png' after your search term. PNG files usually have a transparent background.

→ If you're using Canva to find photos (canva.com/photos/), you can easily select images with a transparent background by adding the word 'isolated' after your search term. For example, 'plastic bottle isolated'.

Tip: put a large image or illustration with a transparent background in the bottom right-hand corner of your poster and arrange the text around it. This works really well.

Put your image on your poster first, and make it big

The image is the first thing you should put on your poster. Researchers often cram their poster full of text, then remember they need to add an image and shove it in a corner somewhere. As the supporting design element on your poster, the image needs to be big. Give it enough space to shine. So make it the first thing you put on your poster. Not the last.

2 Attention

A photo of yourself on your poster?

I'm not a fan of putting a photo of yourself on your poster. It takes away space from the other content and usually doesn't fit with the rest of the poster.

There is an argument that putting your own face on your poster makes it easier for people to find you at the conference. But honestly: does anyone really wade through a whole crowd of people searching for the researcher whose photo they just saw on a poster? Either you're standing next to your poster and then there's no need for your photo, or you're not standing next to your poster but then the audience really isn't going to try and find you in that crowd during the reception. Use the freed-up space to make your contact info more visible. That's far more useful. But we can agree to disagree if you still want to put your own face on your poster. No hard feelings.

Exercise
Look for the perfect image or illustration. Don't settle for the first photo you find. Got the right one? Then put the image on your poster first, before you add the text.

Step 10: Think about your design

A nice design provides clarity, looks professional and helps your audience find the relevant information faster.

1. Colour

Colour guides the eye around a poster. Put *just* your key message in a coloured box, and people will easily find that message among all the other text.

What if your organisation hasn't provided a colour scheme? Don't just mix and match colours that you think look nice. Instead, try out the following tips:

→ **Use a colour wheel.** Color.adobe.com has a colour wheel that helps you find colours that go well together. If you're looking for two colours, complementary shades often work well. You can also upload a photo that you like to the website and Adobe Color will generate a colour palette based on it.

→ **Use the 'Eyedropper'** in, for example, PowerPoint to select a colour on your image and make your titles or boxes the same colour. This is a quick way to tie everything together nicely. In PowerPoint, just select a shape, and you'll find the 'Eyedropper' option under 'Shape Fill'.

Ensure enough colour contrast

Are you using a coloured background for your poster or text box? Then make sure that the text is easy to read. If the background is dark, put your text in white. If it's a light colour, it's best to use black letters. Be careful with combinations like red and green, blue and yellow, blue and purple, and green and blue – people who are colour-blind find it difficult to tell these apart.

Are you working in PowerPoint? Then select a specific colour from your image using the 'Eyedropper'. Other tools often have the same functionality.

We extracted the colours for the boxes on this pitch poster from the image of the orange peel using the 'Eyedropper'.

What is the best background colour to choose?

You might think that a bright background colour like pink or yellow will grab the audience's attention. But it's also guaranteed to make your poster look garish. And after reading two lines of text, your audience will already be wishing they'd brought their sunglasses. A dark background with white letters is often also harder to read. A white background may seem boring, but black text on white is the easiest to read. Add some accent colours by, for example, putting the titles in a different colour or including a colourful image. Giving a few text boxes a coloured background is also another option.

2. Text

How big should your text be?

Visitors should be able to read the main text on your poster from about three metres away. Don't forget to take into account people with impaired vision, or people in wheelchairs who are lower down and, therefore, further away from your poster.

Here are some guidelines based on research for classrooms and signage. Bigger is always better.

Readable from roughly 3 metres
→ Title: 96 pt (or for a short title: 120 pt)
→ Subtitle: 60 pt

Readable from roughly 1.5 metres
→ Headers: 50 pt
→ Body text: 32–40 pt

Readable from roughly 40 cm
→ At least 24 pt. Note that this is the *minimum* font size. So save this for the smallest text on your poster. For example, references (if you're not putting them in your handout). People who are standing further away won't be able to read this. It's too small for your body text.

Resist the temptation to make everything smaller so that all the text fits on your poster. This doesn't do anyone any favours. You may think that everything is perfectly readable, but you're probably sitting half a metre away from your computer screen while you make your poster.

The best way to get an idea of how easy your text is to read is to print out your poster in A4. If you can't read the text, it's too small. Pay specific attention to the smallest text on and around your figures and graphs.

Which font should you use?

We already talked in detail about your organisation's template on page 78. Do they suggest a specific font? Then use that. Don't have a template? Then it's handy to know that fonts are divided into two large groups:

1   **Serif fonts.** A 'serif' is the small line that you see at the top or bottom of letters in certain fonts. <u>Times New Roman</u> is a well-known Serif font, as is <u>Cambria</u>. The dashes guide the eyes through the sentence and have been specially developed for large chunks of text. Open any book and you'll find a serif font. But serif fonts are less suitable for posters and should definitely be avoided for poster titles. They quickly feel dated and weren't meant for shorter pieces of text.
2   **Sans-serif fonts.** These fonts have no dashes at the tops and bottoms of individual letters. They provide a more minimalist, informal and clean look and are better suited to titles. <u>Arial</u> is a sans-serif font. <u>Calibri</u> too. For scientific posters, a sans-serif font is the best choice.

On posters, sans-serif fonts work better than serif fonts.

Steer clear of the more special fonts that you might like but are difficult to read, especially from several metres away. For example:

Edwardian Script

Comic Sans

Jokerman

Only use them for a very specific purpose, like to replicate an unreadable letter (Edwardian Script) or give designers the creeps (Comic Sans). I honestly don't know why you would use Jokerman. Perhaps you're doing research into the psychological benefits of hammocks. Who knows.

3. Give your text room to breathe

One of the most common reasons a poster doesn't look nice or is difficult to read is the amount of space the text has been given on the poster. Often everything is a bit crammed together, or the text is pushed right up against the sides of its box. Let's tackle that in just a few steps.

As the world's largest distributed store of fresh water, ground water plays a central part in sustaining ecosystems and enabling human adaptation to climate variability and change. The strategic importance of ground water for global water and food security will probably intensify under climate change as more frequent and intense climate extremes (droughts and floods) increase variability in precipitation, soil moisture and surface water. Here we critically review recent research assessing the impacts of climate on ground water through natural and human-induced processes as well as through groundwater-driven feedbacks on the climate system. Furthermore, we examine the possible opportunities and challenges of using and sustaining groundwater resources in climate adaptation strategies, and highlight the lack of groundwater observations, which, at present, limits our understanding of the dynamic relationship between ground water and climate.

Step 1. Don't push your text right up against the sides of the text box. This often happens because you've filled the text box itself with a colour. It's better to put a coloured rectangle behind the text.

As the world's largest distributed store of fresh water, ground water plays a central part in sustaining ecosystems and enabling human adaptation to climate variability and change. The strategic importance of ground water for global water and food security will probably intensify under climate change as more frequent and intense climate extremes (droughts and floods) increase variability in precipitation, soil moisture and surface water. Here we critically review recent research assessing the impacts of climate on ground water through natural and human-induced processes as well as through groundwater-driven feedbacks on the climate system. Furthermore, we examine the possible opportunities and challenges of using and sustaining groundwater resources in climate adaptation strategies, and highlight the lack of groundwater observations, which, at present, limits our understanding of the dynamic relationship between ground water and climate.

This is already an improvement, but we can still make it a lot better.

Step 2. Create white space. By splitting your text into paragraphs with an empty line in between, you make it easier to read and faster to scan.

As the world's largest distributed store of fresh water, ground water plays a central part in sustaining ecosystems and enabling human adaptation to climate variability and change.

The strategic importance of ground water for global water and food security will probably intensify under climate change as more frequent and intense climate extremes (droughts and floods) increase variability in precipitation, soil moisture and surface water.

Here we critically review recent research assessing the impacts of climate on ground water through natural and human-induced processes as well as through groundwater-driven feedbacks on the climate system.

Furthermore, we examine the possible opportunities and challenges of using and sustaining groundwater resources in climate adaptation strategies, and highlight the lack of groundwater observations, which, at present, limits our understanding of the dynamic relationship between ground water and climate.

2 Attention

Step 3. Use bold and/or colour to make important words stand out. This makes the text easier to scan.

As the world's largest distributed store of fresh water, ground water plays a central part in sustaining ecosystems and enabling human adaptation to climate variability and change.

The strategic importance of ground water for global water and food security will probably intensify under climate change as more frequent and intense climate extremes (droughts and floods) increase variability in precipitation, soil moisture and surface water.

Here we critically review recent research assessing the impacts of climate on ground water through natural and human-induced processes as well as through groundwater-driven feedbacks on the climate system.

Furthermore, we examine the possible opportunities and challenges of using and sustaining groundwater resources in climate adaptation strategies, and highlight the lack of groundwater observations, which, at present, limits our understanding of the dynamic relationship between ground water and climate.

Step 4. Organise the text into columns. Posters are big sheets of paper, and it's difficult to read sentences or paragraphs that run from left to right across the entire poster. This applies to a portrait poster, but even more so to a landscape poster. Use columns to make it easier to read.

As the world's largest distributed store of fresh water, ground water plays a central part in sustaining ecosystems and enabling human adaptation to climate variability and change.

The strategic importance of ground water for global water and food security will probably intensify under climate change as more frequent and intense climate extremes (droughts and floods) increase variability in precipitation, soil moisture and surface water.

Here we critically review recent research assessing the impacts of climate on ground water through natural and human-induced processes as well as through groundwater-driven feedbacks on the climate system.

Furthermore, we examine the possible opportunities and challenges of using and sustaining groundwater resources in climate adaptation strategies, and highlight the lack of groundwater observations, which, at present, limits our understanding of the dynamic relationship between ground water and climate.

Step 5. Use descriptive headers. In the example below, the audience only needs to read three headers to know what it's about. So make sure you use descriptive headers. Don't write 'Introduction'. Instead, tell us what we need to remember. In this example: 'Groundwater is important.' Compare the reworked version below with the first version where the text was squished up against the sides of the box. It's much easier to read and looks a lot more professional too.

Groundwater is important
As the world's largest distributed store of fresh water, ground water plays a central part in sustaining ecosystems and enabling human adaptation to climate variability and change.

The strategic importance of ground water for global water and food security will probably intensify under climate change as more frequent and intense climate extremes (droughts and floods) increase variability in precipitation, soil moisture and surface water.

We reviewed the research
Here we critically review recent research assessing the impacts of climate on ground water through natural and human-induced processes as well as through groundwater-driven feedbacks on the climate system.

There is a lack of observations
Furthermore, we examine the possible opportunities and challenges of using and sustaining groundwater resources in climate adaptation strategies, and highlight the lack of groundwater observations, which, at present, limits our understanding of the dynamic relationship between ground water and climate.

4. Keep it simple

Don't add anything that will only make the design of your poster busier or more complicated. For example, shadows, reflections, 3D text or other elements. PowerPoint has several funky effect settings that you can go to town with on your images. But as a rule, you're best off leaving these well alone. Or in the words of a well-known design principle: perfection is when you have nothing to take away.

Reflection, rotation, 3D text effects.
Leave them well alone. Keep it simple.

5. The ideal size and the best orientation

You can always expect to receive poster guidelines from the conference containing – hopefully – the required poster size. A1 (big) and A0 (very big) are the most common. You will rarely come across A2 or A3. Never print your poster smaller than the requested size because a small poster is less noticeable, and the text more difficult to read.

This poster was made in A2, but could just as easily have been A1, twice the size.

I regularly receive poster designs that were created in PowerPoint's standard 16:9 slide format. These are not the right dimensions for a poster and a printer can't print them in a large size. Are you making a poster in PowerPoint? Then adjust the dimensions of your slide before you start. To do this, go to Design >> Slide Size >> Custom Slide Size and set the correct dimensions.

Here are the standard dimensions:
→ A0: 118.9 cm x 84.1 cm
→ A1: 84.1 cm x 59.4 cm

Once you know how big your poster can be, should you choose a landscape or portrait orientation? This has probably already been decided by the conference. But if you're not sure, portrait is generally the safest bet. Simply because most poster panels at conferences cater to portrait posters.

If it's not in the guidelines, ask in advance about the dimensions and orientation of the poster panels. It would be a shame for all your hard work to go to waste just because your poster doesn't fit on the panel.

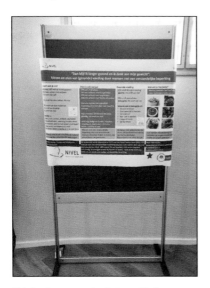

This landscape poster is too wide for the panel.

And this portrait poster is too long. People have to bend down to read the bottom. Check the dimensions before you start!

6. What is the best tool to use?

The ideal tool for creating scientific posters all comes down to personal preference, but here are a few options:

PowerPoint: The vast majority of researchers use PowerPoint to create their posters, which is absolutely fine. PowerPoint has the big advantage that you're probably already familiar with it. You know how to add text boxes, insert images, and make text bigger or smaller. So you can dive straight in. Always export your poster to PDF before sending it to a printer.

Canva.com: This is an online tool for creating beautiful designs, from flyers to videos, but also posters. Canva has a lot of ready-made elements, poster templates, photos, icons and colour schemes, so it's a big help when it comes to your design. It has a free and a paid version, but the free version is perfectly fine and definitely worth trying out if you're struggling with your poster design. Many of the most attractive posters I come across these days have been made in Canva. If only it could help you with the content too…

Adobe InDesign: InDesign is an Adobe program for creating graphic files like flyers, leaflets and posters. Unfortunately, it's also an expensive tool with a steep learning curve. So it only makes sense to choose this tool if you already have an Adobe package on your computer or some experience with similar Adobe software, like Photoshop or Illustrator.

LaTeX: Some researchers use LaTeX because it's very good at displaying mathematical formulas. But for making a poster, I wouldn't recommend it. Posters made in LaTeX often look very programmed. Still need a nice way to present a mathematical formula? Then create the formula in LaTeX and export it to another tool.

More tools are available. As long as they're easy to use, you can create a nice poster with them, and if they can export that poster to PDF, you can't go far wrong.

7. Where to have your poster printed?

Your organisation probably has its own copy shop where you can have posters printed. Usually at a discounted rate or even for free. Otherwise, there are all kinds of printers (online and in a shop) that will be able to help you.

Researchers are increasingly printing their posters on fabric. You can easily pack it into your suitcase and afterwards reuse it as a tablecloth or turn it into a tote bag. Whether you choose paper or fabric is a personal choice. Paper is less harmful for the environment and easier to recycle and hang up with tape, and offers the added advantage that you won't need to iron it the day before your poster presentation.

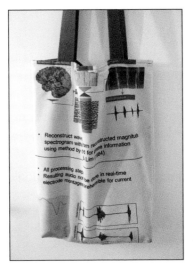

Christian Herff later turned his fabric poster into a tote bag.

8. Don't forget to add your contact info

One of the things I have to repeat the most during feedback sessions is: 'Don't forget to add your contact info.' If the whole point of having a poster is to help you network, start conversations and possibly work together with other researchers later on, then they need to be able to find you.

Clearly display your contact info (name and email is usually enough) on the poster. Where exactly you put it depends on the poster itself, but bottom right is a logical choice. Institution logos are also best off placed in the footer rather than at the top where you often see them. Most visitors aren't primarily interested in which institution did the research, so it's a shame if those logos steal away the top spot from your title.

9. Good headers are important

Words like 'introduction' or 'results' don't make for particularly informative headers on a poster. It's often better to use more descriptive headers. These immediately convey the message and make your poster easier to scan. To come up with a good header, ask yourself what the key message of that specific block on your poster is. For example, are you doing research into the quality of heroin?

→   Instead of 'Introduction' as a header, use: 'Heroin needs a quality label'
→   Instead of 'Results' as a header, use: '13% heroin in a sample'

Exercise
Work your way through the tips above. Is there anything you can already do to improve your poster?

Step 11: Bring in your data

Data is the golden nugget of your research, the thing you've spent so long working towards. So a graph is often the first thing people look at on your poster. But no matter how fascinating your data is, a dry table or summary of figures won't stick in anyone's mind. And simply taking a screenshot of your Excel graph doesn't work either. So how should you present your data?

How to create a powerful graph for your poster?

A whole course on data visualisation is beyond the scope of this book, but we'd still like to share some tips on how to create powerful graphs. Because if you design them well, they can be real powerhouses that help shine a light on some complex topics.

The three examples below were developed by Koen Van den Eeckhout. Koen is an ex-researcher who, together with his company Baryon, helps researchers and companies visualise their data clearly. His extensive book about data visualisation (*Powerful Charts*) is full of great examples and surprising insights. We definitely recommend reading it if you want to dig deeper into the topic. For your poster, we want you to think about the following things in particular.

1. Put the conclusion in the graph title

There is a lot you can do with your graphs, but the most important tip is: put the conclusion you want your audience to remember in the title of the graph. We often see quite vague titles like 'This is experiment X with sample Y'. This means your audience has to analyse the entire graph themselves and draw their own conclusions from the data. But they don't know as much about your topic as you do, and there's a good chance they'll draw the wrong conclusions or not even bother.

Help them out by putting the graph's key conclusion in the title. For example, 'Doing Y causes X to peak.' Also be as specific as possible in your verbal explanation. Don't say, 'in this figure we can see the key result', because then people stop listening to you and start analysing the graph. Instead, say: 'this graph shows that doing Y causes X to peak.' This means they don't need to analyse the graph themselves while you're still talking.

Take the example below about meat consumption in the US. The graph is nicely presented and shows the data, but has no clear message and leaves the audience having to do all the thinking themselves.

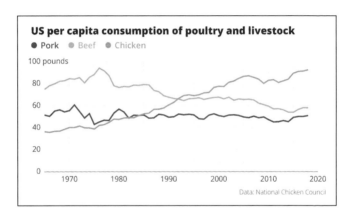

Here is the same graph, but with a few changes:

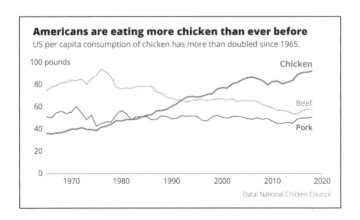

The key message – the graph's conclusion – is now in the title and is immediately clear: Americans are eating more chicken than ever before. With a clever use of colour, we've reinforced that message even more. The two lines for beef and pork are now grey, so they fade into the background, and the line for chicken gets a bright accent colour.

2. Think about your audience!

Think carefully about who will be looking at your graph, because if your audience doesn't understand it, there's no point in including it. Let's say you did research into luminous materials and you present your results to an audience of interior designers, hospital managers and materials experts. If the graph you put on your poster is lifted straight from your most recent publication, it's not going to have the desired effect.

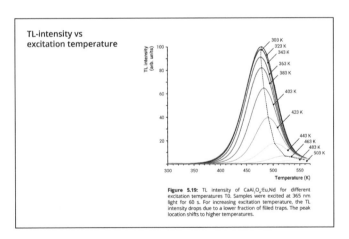

Figure 5.19: TL intensity of $CaAl_2O_4$:Eu,Nd for different excitation temperatures T0. Samples were excited at 365 nm light for 60 s. For increasing excitation temperature, the TL intensity drops due to a lower fraction of filled traps. The peak location shifts to higher temperatures.

This is the kind of graph that you often see at a poster fair. It's difficult to read quickly with all its jargon, abbreviations and crammed-in text. A lot of your audience will likely ignore your graph, or even decide to move on to someone else's poster.

Before creating your graph, ask yourself the following questions:

→ **What decision** do you want your audience to make, and what data should you show to help them get there?

→ **How much time** will they spend looking at your graph? The most important things should be immediately clear.

A better version of our graph would look like this:

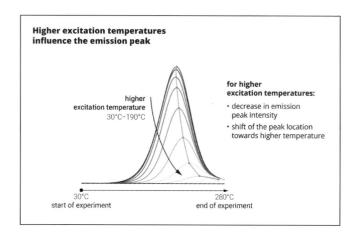

We now have less text and no more abbreviations or jargon. This makes it quicker and easier for the audience to read. Also note that we put the key message of the graph in the title. This means your audience doesn't even need to look at the graph to grasp the most important information.

3. Limit the noise

The correct signal-to-noise ratio is important in a graph. Our key message or conclusion is the signal we want to send out, so that's what we want to make as clear as possible. And the noise? This is anything on our graph that gets in the way of that. Do you see anything on your graph that you can leave out without taking away from the key message? That's noise!

The following graph contains a lot of noise:

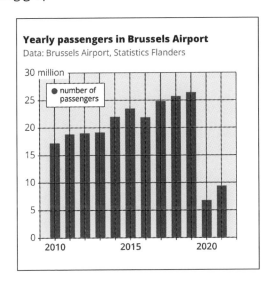

We can easily leave out a few things, like the grey background, grid lines, key and even the axis lines!

Here's how it looks now:

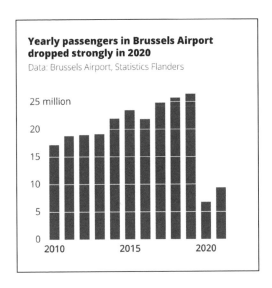

The graph is a lot clearer without the noise. Removing noise doesn't necessarily have to mean deleting elements from the graph. Sometimes you also need to add things to make the conclusion more obvious. In the example about chicken consumption in the US, the eye-catching red accent colour pushes the noise to the background and the key message to the foreground.

In summary, a powerful graph needs to:
1   have a title that conveys a clear message,
2   be useful for your audience, and
3   contain limited noise.

Applying these three principles will ensure that the graphs on your next poster are inspiring and convincing.

The font-focused chart is your friend

You don't always have to use graphs. Another option that also works very well on a poster is a font-focused chart.

Font-focused charts look professional and are really easy to create. Simply put the number in a large font, then add a few words and an icon.

4200
VACCINES
ADMINISTERED

WE CAN MAINTAIN
150
MEANINGFUL
RELATIONSHIPS

Font-focused charts grab the audience's attention and are ideal for highlighting a specific number. They are popular because they make people feel like they've learnt something interesting in a short space of time.

There are two font-focused charts on this poster, to the right of the image. They are a useful way to quickly convey an important number and grab the audience's attention (poster by Salvatore Ciano).

Use a timeline for processes or plans

Do you have a process or step-by-step plan that you'd like to display clearly on your poster? Then draw a timeline. The simplest approach is to draw a line and plot the bubbles or steps along it in the correct order. Add some icons and colours, and it quickly turns your poster into a real eye-catcher.

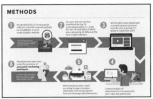

A timeline is ideal for clearly displaying processes or plans, and makes a nice change from a block of text.

Tables aren't always necessary

Before you put a table on your poster, ask yourself: does all that data need to be on the poster? Or do you just want to highlight the conclusion of the table? If it's just about the conclusion, or a selection of the data in the table, then put only that conclusion or selection on your poster and move the full table to your handout.

The example below is a table from a poster about research into the most popular communication channel per age group. The researcher was mainly interested in which communication channel young people use. If that's your goal, then you don't need the columns for over-40s to make your point. We can tell that the researcher had already identified the relevant data because he put a red box around it. If the red boxes contain the most relevant numbers, keep only those.

Social media use per age category

% use	15-19 years old	20-39 years old	40-64 years old	65-79 years old	80+ years old
	97%	92%	85%	63%	35%
	69%	77%	80%	61%	61%
	89%	86%	57%	41%	24%
	15%	48%	38%	16%	10%
	78%	49%	25%	11%	9%
	20%	29%	23%	11%	9%
	21%	32%	23%	16%	11%
	90%	35%	10%	1%	1%

This table contains too much data that isn't needed to understand the message. In fact, the amount of data provided actually makes it harder to understand.

The following reworked version of the table fits much better on a poster, attracts more attention and communicates the important data more clearly. Also note the key message in the title. This means that visitors don't have to interpret the data themselves and will definitely come to the right conclusion.

% use	15-19 years old	20-39 years old
	97%	92%
	69%	77%
	89%	86%
	78%	49%
	90%	35%

WhatsApp is the most popular communication service **among both teenagers and young adults**

Put only the most relevant data on your poster. It is now immediately clear that WhatsApp is the most popular communication channel.

2 Attention

Exercise

Look critically at your data. Do you really need everything on your poster? What can you get rid of? Is there a number that you can turn into a font-focused chart? Is the conclusion of each graph or table included in the title?

Step 12: Add an element of surprise

Do you really want your poster to stand out? Then think about how you could add an element of surprise. This will have a big impact.

1. Bring a prop

Is there something that would make your research tangible or visually represent it? Then bring that along to the poster fair and show it to people. Are you doing research into skin brighteners? Then bring the beauty products with you. Are you researching a new type of fire extinguisher? Then show it. Are you looking into specific books, developing a new app, making ink for a 3D printer that prints tissues, or researching the cocoa bean? A physical object will immediately grab people's attention.

Imagine a whole row of posters and in front of one of them a table with a collection of objects. Where do you think people are going to stop? At the table, of course. Or at the very least, they'll take a quick look.

You don't always have to bring along the actual research materials. How about a cuddly toy of the E. coli bacteria or the gallbladder (both of which you can buy at giantmicrobes.com), a jar of water from a local river to introduce your story about water pollution, or the pile of books children have to carry in their rucksacks to school every day and that leads to back problems? Or are you an engineer researching timber-frame buildings? Then have your audience build something with wooden sticks. Let your imagination run wild. This is a great way to grab the audience's attention and get conversations started.

Oh, so you really are researching cocoa beans? A top tip: hand out chocolate next to your poster, and you'll hands down win the award for the most conversations that day. But isn't that cheating? No, because you are actually doing research into chocolate, and you're talking about cocoa beans while they're eating them. Those few chocolates will be the best investment you'll make for the entire conference. And by extension, the same tip goes for anyone doing any kind of food research, from insect crisps to drought-resistant rice.

2. Get creative with your poster

Who says a poster has to be just a boring sheet of paper? See what you can conjure up with some scissors, tape and creativity.

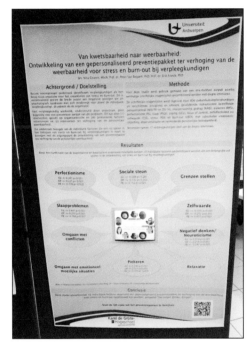

In this example, the researcher cut a hole in her poster to stick an iPad in it. Visitors could use the iPad to select and listen to different testimonials.

Or how about this pull-out card on which researcher Diana Széliová wrote the mathematical formulas that only experts would be interested in? If they wanted to know more, they just had to pull out the card. (Also note here the really clear key message at the top of the poster.)

Poster with pull-out card by Diana Széliová.

Or what about a 3D poster about 3D research I once saw? Next to the poster there was a pair of 3D glasses on a string. Everyone wanted to try it out, of course.

I once stuck several possible questions on bits of paper next to my poster underneath the words: 'Questions you can ask me.' And you guessed it, most of the questions I got asked came from there. At a conference on higher education in Cuba, my colleague Hans placed a sheet of paper next to his poster to ask the audience's opinion on a statement. This got so much response that some Cuban research-ers even wrote a paper about it based on that input.

2 Attention

By placing a paper for feedback next to his poster, Hans collected so many responses that Cuban researchers wrote a paper about it.

But you can think even bigger than this. Why not do something with pieces of Velcro that people can use to stick words in the right place? Or with strings to connect different concepts to each other?

Or make question-and-answer flaps on your poster. Write the ques-tion on the front and the answer on the back.

By getting creative with your poster, you turn it into an interactive event where there's something for people to really experience. Give them an activity, and they'll never forget your poster.

3. Hand something out

We already talked about the power of handouts in step 6 on page 57: they give you somewhere to put all the info that doesn't fit on your poster. But there are also other things you can give away to your audience, like:

→   A survey to fill in
→   Tear-off slips with your contact info or a link
→   A business card
→   An A4 print-out of your poster
→   A project brochure

You could also have postcards printed with a nice photo of what you're researching (or of a crop, book, machine, etc. that you're using in your work) or your key message. Don't forget to add your contact info and perhaps also a link or QR code.

Postcards or handouts placed on, around or next to a poster stand out from the crowd. Anyone who is interested will be happy to take one with them and, after the event, they'll have a physical reminder of your research that will often sit on their desk for a long time. This keeps you top of mind, which is exactly what you were after, right?

4. Social media

If the event has a hashtag, use it to promote your poster. Take a photo of yourself next to your poster, add a short title and your conference location, and post it on social media using the hashtag. Visitors usually keep a close eye on event hashtags. How else do you think we found the poster with pull-out card?

By sharing this photo of her poster with pull-out card on social media, Diana Széliová drew a bigger audience and made it into our book.

Exercise
Look at the previous tips and let your creativity run wild. Is there something you can bring along or give away? Can you add an element of surprise to your poster?

2. Attention

Another alternative: the Better Poster Design.

In addition to the pitch poster and the expert poster, there is a third type of poster we'd like to share with you: the Better Poster, an idea developed by researcher Mike Morrison. His first design went viral on YouTube thanks to a cool video, and since then he's developed a second design. A Better Poster looks like this:

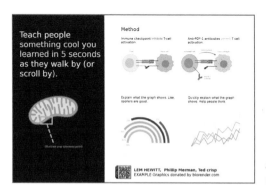

An example of a Better Poster.

The key elements are:

1   A large key message with a supporting image.
2   Some graphs or figures to help you tell your story.
3   A QR code for more info.

Morrison recommends creating a poster that you can read and analyse from a short distance in 30 seconds. Definitely a powerful approach and fun to experiment with. Want to watch the Better Poster Design videos that went viral? Then search for 'Better Poster Mike Morrison' on YouTube. They're really well made. If you want to dig deeper, check out the referenced studies in the video notes. Mike Morrison has made Better Poster Design templates available here: https://osf.io/6ua4k

Step 13: Ask for feedback

The best way to make your poster even better? Ask for feedback. But if you're asking for that feedback from your colleagues, you'll need two things:

1 Honest colleagues who aren't afraid to say if it's not good.
2 A mindset that is open to feedback. Take all the feedback on board and don't get defensive.

A good way to approach this is not to be there when your colleagues give their feedback. Print out your poster a month before the conference and put it up in the corridor. Leave a stack of post-it notes next to it, and ask people to write down their feedback and stick it on the poster. If you stand next to your poster like a proud parent, your colleagues often won't dare to say more than 'what a great poster', but if you give them the time to look at the poster and form their own opinion without you looking over their shoulder, their feedback will be honest and valuable.

Does printing out your poster, hanging it up and providing post-it notes all sound like too much hassle? Then simply ask your colleagues for feedback while they look at a projection of your poster, or send them the PDF and ask them to add their comments to the file.

Feedback is always welcome but keep the following limitations in mind!

1 Your colleagues may not be representative of the target audience you want to reach at the conference. There is a good chance they already know your research and the jargon used, and will therefore be focused on what you've missed out,

2 Attention

encouraging you to add more info. If your goal is to reach people who aren't yet familiar with your research, it's better to ask for feedback not from your immediate colleagues but from people who don't know what you do exactly. Someone from another research group, for example.

2　Keep in mind that at a poster fair there's not just one, but hundreds of posters. The people you ask feedback from may take the time to look at everything in detail, while at a poster fair they would only have time to give it a quick glance. That's why it's a good idea to ask them to initially look at the poster for just 30 seconds. Then they have to tell you what grabbed their attention and whether they already know what the key message is. After that, they can go through the whole poster again in more detail.

Exercise

Take a moment to think about who you could ask for feedback and how you would go about it.

Should heroin carry a quality label?

Concern for fentanyl-laced heroin negated through the RADAR-heroin-23 project

M. Balcaen[1], M. Degreef[1], E. Deconinck[2], L. Gremeaux[1]

1. Unit Illicit Drugs, Sciensano, Brussels, Belgium • 2. Medicines and Health Products, Sciensano, Brussels, Belgium

QUALITY NOT GUARANTEED

Should we focus more on the uncertainties of heroin's drug quality?

Example 1
Data from seizures doesn't always reflect the quality of drugs sold on the streets.[1]

Example 2
Fentanyl-laced heroin at origin of several deaths in Melbourne, Australia.[2]

Example 3
Intoxications caused by heroin adulterated with synthetic cannabinoid, 5F-MDMB-PINACA.[3]

Need for more up-to-date information on the quality of street level heroin in Belgium.

Questionnaire

A survey conducted amongst people who use heroin, questioning details of purchase and the experienced effects after consuming heroin

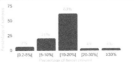

N = 128

Analysis of street heroin

Quantitative and qualitative analysis, with GC-MS and LC-DAD, **of street level heroin** received from people who completed the questionnaire

PURCHASE & PRICE

81% PURCHASED HEROIN THROUGH A DEALER

0% PURCHASED HEROIN ONLINE

€10/gr. MIN. — €83/gr. MAX.

€21.6 AVERAGE PRICE PER GRAM OF HEROIN

PURITY

ON AVERAGE **13% HEROIN** IN A STREET SAMPLE

Percentage of heroin present: [0.2-5%], [5-10%], [10-20%], [20-30%], ≥30%

CONSUMPTION & EXPERIENCE

64% SMOKES HEROIN

34% INJECTS HEROIN

5.5 OUT OF 10 WAS THE AVERAGE SCORE FOR QUALITY

7% EXPERIENCED UNEXPECTED EFFECTS

ADULTERANTS

Acetaminophen 95%
Diacetamate 95%
Caffeine 92%
Cocaine 7%
Bromazepam 1%
Pseudococaine 1%
Ketamine 1%

96% OF SAMPLES HAS AT LEAST ONE ADULTERANT

NO FENTANYL OR ANALOGUE WAS DETECTED

LESSONS LEARNED

INVOLVEMENT OF PEOPLE WHO USE HEROIN
· Purchase method and consumption patterns of street level heroin
· Information on perceived quality
· Experience with unexpected effects

REGULAR ANALYSIS OF STREET SAMPLES
· More accurate estimation of the quality of street level heroin
· Presence of adulterants
· Relation price and purity

Want to receive the article when available?

Sciensano · Balcaen, Margot · margot.balcaen@sciensano.be · T: +32 471 73 15 44 · www.sciensano.be

Balcaen:
1. Evrard I, Legleye S, Cadet-Taïrou A. Composition, purity and perceived quality of street cocaine in France. International Journal of Drug Policy. 2010 Sep 1;21(5):399–406.
2. Rodda LN, Pilgrim JL, Di Rago M, Crump K, Gerostamoulos D, Drummer OH. A Cluster of Fentanyl-Laced Heroin Deaths in 2015 in Melbourne, Australia. Journal of Analytical Toxicology. 2017 May 1;41(4):318–24.
3. Ershad M, Deiv Cruz M, Mostafa A, Khalid MM, Arnold R, Hamilton R. Heroin Adulterated with the Novel Synthetic Cannabinoid, 5F-MDMB-PINACA: A Case Series. Clin Pract Cases Emerg Med. 2020 Apr 23;4(2):121–5.

.be

A nice poster with a lot of strong elements and a few things that could make it even better. You can read our feedback on the next two pages (poster by Margot Balcaen).

Feedback on a poster

Margot Balcaen, a researcher at Sciensano, made a poster after attending one of our workshops. What works very well about this poster is:

→ **The title 'Should heroin carry a quality label?'** The title is a clear question that grabs the audience's attention. The subtitle is a scientific explanation, but you can ignore it if it contains too much jargon for you.

→ **The stamp 'quality not guaranteed'** in the top right-hand corner grabs our attention and also makes the problem immediately clear.

→ **The first header** is 'Should we focus more on the uncertainties of heroin's drug quality?' A pertinent question. A lot of researchers would put something like 'Introduction' here, but that tells us very little. It's better to use more descriptive headers or, as in this case, a question.

→ **Font-focused charts:** Margot made some beautiful font-focused charts. Like in the 'Purchase & Price' box, which immediately gives you the key numbers. If you were to write those numbers out in full sentences, it would be much harder to read.

→ **The graphs** in the bottom right – 'Purity' and 'Adulterants' – are nicely designed in the colours of the poster and the graph titles clearly contain the main message ('On average 13% heroin in a street sample').

→ **The lessons learned.** The very clear 'lessons learned' icon makes it impossible to miss the key conclusions.

→ She ends with her **contact details and a QR code**. That QR code takes you to a form where you can leave your details if you want to receive the full paper once it's available. A smart approach for researchers who haven't yet finished their paper. The visitors who fill in that form are worth their weight in gold: these are the people you can start projects with later on or who you will often bump into at future conferences.

→ She uses a consistent **colour scheme** throughout the poster, which ties everything together nicely, and has used the icons well.

Some example tips to make it even better:

→ She could **rework the title** into a statement instead of a question: 'Heroin should carry a quality label.' This is more powerful.

→ The poster has a nice design, but there's little that really grabs your attention. **A large photo** of, for example, a hypodermic needle or a bag of heroin would attract even more attention, but she would need to make sure that it still fits with the rest of the poster.

→ The 'lessons learned' block is nice and clear, but I still don't see a **prominently placed key message**. This can be easily fixed by putting 'involvement of people who use heroin' and 'regular analysis of street samples' in a green box at the bottom. She could also rework it into a clear statement and make that more obvious: 'We need to involve people who use heroin and do a regular analysis of street samples.'

2 Attention

PART 3
At the conference

It took blood, sweat and tears to get here, and now you're standing next to your poster at the conference. People are walking by and glancing at what you made from a distance, but that's usually as close as they get. Then someone approaches. They carefully read your poster. 'This is my chance,' you think. But what should you do? What should you say?

Lots of researchers stand next to their posters, unsure of what to say and waiting for the visitor to speak to them. But that doesn't work. **It's your job to get the conversation started. It's up to you to break the ice.** If you wait for the other person, you'll only speak to extroverts who are also very sure of themselves. So you have to make the first move.

Key insight

It's your job as the researcher to get the conversation started. It's up to you to break the ice.

———

We previously described how to write a good one-minute pitch (step 3, page 40). If you use that short pitch in your opening conversation, you'll already be doing better than almost everyone else, but of course you shouldn't just launch into your pitch as soon as someone stops at your poster. There's something you need to do first: ask a question.

Step 14: Think of an icebreaker question

─────

A recognisable or surprising question linked to your research is the perfect way to start the conversation and break the ice. For example, ask:

→ 'Do you know at which stage of your life you're most likely to develop depression?'
→ to which the person in front of you can answer either 'yes', 'no' or 'I'm not sure',
→ to which you can say: 'It's a difficult one. Did you know that elderly people in nursing homes are twice as likely to develop depression? That has to change, and luckily this is what my research is all about,' after which you take the person to your poster or start the short one-minute pitch you prepared earlier.

Asking a question is an easy way to make contact and start a conversation about your poster. And it also gives you the chance to assess the person's background. If you ask, 'Can bioplastic pens be thrown on the compost heap?' and they come up with an answer about which microorganisms and temperature they think would be most suitable for industrial composting, then you know you'll have to give this person a different explanation than someone who has never heard of compostable bioplastics.

Always think of a question that your audience can answer. For example, if you ask, 'Do you think it is possible for formally different constructions to express one and the same function?' Then my only answer is 'What? I don't understand the question.' And then of course it doesn't work. Instead, a clear question that also gets the person interested is the ideal way to start a meaningful conversation.

Should you latch onto everyone who comes within ten metres of your poster? No. Choose only the people who show a bit of interest in your poster, the person who lingers a little longer and who you think might have read the title and also perhaps looked at a graph. Don't be pushy, and always be polite. Start by saying, 'Can I ask you something?' People usually respond with a hesitant 'Um... yes.' That's your green light to ask the icebreaker question you've prepared, after which you continue the conversation.

Some will answer you with a firm 'no'. Definitely don't take this personally. Perhaps they're short on time, have to get to a presentation or simply need a bathroom break. Wish them a nice day, and end the conversation with a friendly smile. That's totally fine, because there's nothing more annoying than talking to someone who doesn't actually want to listen to you.

Having an icebreaker question ready **is one of our top tips for good poster presentations**. Come up with several questions so that you can vary them throughout the day. This also keeps it more interesting for you.

Exercise
What question are you going to ask your audience? How will you help your visitor relate to your poster or research?

How to talk to people

Talk mainly to people you don't already know

It's easily done. You're at a poster session, either as a visitor or a presenter, and you look out for the people you already know:

colleagues, for example, or researchers from other institutions who met once at a workshop. You already have something in common, which makes it easier to get the conversation started. But this isn't a good idea. You may be starting conversations, but they're not the kind of conversations that lead to new opportunities.

Bite the bullet and talk mainly to people you don't already know. You have to take the first step.

Give the visitor a little space: find out their interests and background

Once the conversation has started and you've asked your ice-breaker question, go in search of the person's background as quickly as possible. Feel free to follow up with an additional question like: 'Before I explain, may I ask what your background is?' or: 'Was there something specific that attracted you to this topic? Then I'll know what to focus on in my explanation.' Remember to tailor the rest of your talk accordingly.

Most people who stop at your poster do so for a reason, and it's up to you to find out what that reason is before you start your explanation. Maybe they're doing the same research, using the same method, or attended the same university ten years ago and want to know if a specific professor is still teaching there. You don't know what your audience is looking for until you ask. Based on the answer they give, you can start the right conversation or pitch. Simply launching into your standard explanation of the method you used like an overexcited puppy makes little sense if they only want to know which partners you work with.

Remember: you're at the poster fair to have conversations, not to dump information. In many poster sessions you see researchers engage in an enthusiastic conversation, but then at a certain point they switch to presentation mode and start rattling off their standard poster pitch like a robot

What a shame, because this is how you lose the valuable connection you were building up. So make sure you stay in conversation mode the whole time. Create space for your visitor to respond and ask questions. This keeps the conversation going and makes it easier for you to tell when the person is losing interest. Have they stopped asking questions or are their eyes glazing over? Then it's time to wrap up. A concluding question like 'Is there anything else you would like to know?' is better than 'Was everything clear?' People will almost always answer the latter with 'yes'.

Your body language speaks volumes

I remember a poster fair where a certain poster had caught my eye. Unfortunately, the author of the poster was sitting on a table, with her back towards me, talking to her colleague who had been there the whole time.

You would expect the creator of the poster to tell her story with great enthusiasm, but that's not what happened. When I asked her something, she turned around, and her face said it all: she was bored out of her mind. And so she missed the opportunity to really inspire someone with her research.

If you want people to approach you, make sure your body language is inviting. This means:

1   Smile. You'll come across as friendly and enthusiastic.
2   Make eye contact. It's much easier to start a conversation this way. But don't stare at people either. That makes them

uncomfortable. I know, it's tricky trying to find the right balance of 'just enough' eye contact, especially as it's different for everyone.

3   Stand up straight and never cross your arms or hands. An open posture indicates that you're open to talking and a straight back radiates self-confidence. One option to avoid crossing your arms or putting your hands in your pockets is to hold something in your hand. A pen, for example. This also allows you to point out things on your poster.

Nervous? Your poster is the ideal diversion

We understand that not everyone likes talking to complete strangers. But a poster fair is mostly a social event. Are you nervous or finding it all a bit stressful? Then remember that your poster is the ideal diversion. If it's well made, people will be looking at your poster, taking the pressure off you. If you have an object, like a bottle of oil that you can show people while you talk about your research on vegetable fats, then that's something else they can focus on. And it might also help you keep your nerves under control.

It's also important to remember that people aren't at a poster fair to judge you. They're looking for interesting information and great conversations. Usually, they are researchers who are in exactly the same boat as you. Sometimes they're unsure, especially if they're at the beginning of their research. So it's safe to let go of that fear that you're being judged.

How to handle people coming and going

Not everyone will arrive at your poster at the same time, but rather trickle in and out. While you're talking to one person, another person will join you halfway through your conversation. A bit later on, the second person may have left, but a group of three people will take their place. What's the best way to handle that?

It depends on when the new people arrive.

→   Have you only just started? Then you can probably start over.
→   Are you halfway through your explanation? Then finish explaining before repeating it to the newcomers. Unless those newcomers are really important (the five-person jury for the all-important poster award, for example). In that case, apologise to the original person, and let them know you're going to start the explanation again from the top.
→   Almost at the end of your talk? Then let the newcomer know, and wrap up the initial conversation first.

Whatever you do, always briefly acknowledge that someone new has arrived. Some people deliberately listen in on other conversations so that they get the info without having to talk to you personally. Others will wait their turn, but if you don't acknowledge their arrival and your conversation with the other person goes on too long, they'll eventually wander off. Adopting approachable body language with a simple 'hi' or 'welcome', a smile and eye contact, or turning slightly so that the new person can join the circle, goes a long way.

Had a good conversation? Then ask for contact info

A small but crucial tip: did you click with someone? Then ask for their contact details so you can email them after the conference or connect with them on professional social media like LinkedIn.

Specific Situations

1. How to win a poster contest?

Conferences regularly organise poster contests where a jury chooses their favourite poster. Sometimes there is also an audience award. You typically need to indicate in advance if you want to enter, and prizes vary from 'for the honour' to a cash prize that will roughly cover your costs to attend the conference. Winning a poster contest is great. It looks good on your CV, is a real motivation booster, and shines an even brighter light on your research. If you get the chance, definitely take part.

That being said, it's important to know that:
1   It's not always the best posters that win.
2   Winning an award shouldn't be the main reason to attend a poster fair. Interaction and meaningful conversations are more important. Winning a prize is just the cherry on top.

With that in mind, taking part in a poster contest adds an extra dimension to your conference experience. Simply knowing that your poster is being judged will motivate you to think harder about your poster and your talk, and as a result you'll come up with a better poster.

Know what the jury is looking for

If you're taking part in a poster contest, it's useful to know what the jury is looking for as part of their assessment. The most efficient way to find out is to look for the guidelines that the jury gets to evaluate your poster. Found them? Bingo! You now know exactly what the jury will be looking for. Can't find anything? Then ask the

organisers or search online for 'Poster score sheet', preferably together with a search term that's as close as you can get to the conference topic.

Once you know what the jury is looking for, you can use that to your
advantage. Are they interested in your method or are they mainly
looking for social relevance? How many points will they award for
the oral presentation? Unfortunately, that's where things sometimes get tricky: the jury isn't always looking for the best scientific
poster. For example, the scorecard might say: 'Is there an abstract?'
Putting an abstract on a poster is a stupid idea and really makes no
sense, but if 15% of the points are going to be allocated to the abstract, it's probably a good idea to include one.

So don't get demotivated if you made a fantastic poster but still
didn't win a prize: it could have simply been down to some irrele-
vant judging criteria. This also explains why the best posters often
win the audience award rather than the jury prize.

It needs to be crystal clear

When it comes to a poster contest, simply attracting attention
isn't enough. That's what you do to get the audience to stop at
your poster, but the jury is going to stop at your poster anyway. In a
poster contest, it's all about the content and how clearly you convey it. What is your key message? What problem are you tackling?
How did you conduct your research? Why is it relevant? So the design is less important here. But certainly don't see that as a green
light to produce the traditional wall-full-of-text poster. On the con-
trary, it's an invitation to think even harder about how to present
your research in a crystal-clear way.

Make sure they remember your poster

If you're number 14 of 50 posters that the jury will be looking at, it's even more important to stand out. It's a bit like the entry number 7 at the Eurovision Song Contest, which you can never remember by the end of the night. The jury members may jot down a few thoughts on a notepad or scorecard, but they only make their final decision after looking at all of the posters. And despite the scorecard, that final decision is often based on a gut feeling or whichever one they remember the most when they come to their deliberations. So make sure that it's your poster that sticks in the jury's mind. Even 50 posters later.

To achieve this, it's important to realise that in a poster contest, it isn't your poster that does most of the work, but you. Getting into the jury's head is going to require more than just data and results. Although tangible results and interesting research are important, there will always be someone at the poster fair whose research was more interesting. Depending on the number of posters they have to judge, the jury members probably won't have time to review and discuss each area of your research in detail.

The way to stand out in a poster contest is mainly through your conversation. This might even be more important than the poster itself. Was it a smooth conversation that was easy to follow, and do the jury members get how relevant and fascinating your research is? Then you're in with a chance. Of course, the poster is still very important. Know your poster inside out, and make sure you understand and can explain everything on it. Also ensure that your title and graphs are clear and that you have an eye-catching image. Consider bringing a prop along too. If you can combine a clear conversation with a creative poster, you'll be well on your way. Good luck!

2. How to approach an online poster presentation?

Online poster presentations usually work as follows: during a video call you share your poster with the other attendees and give a short explanation. An alternative approach is to pre-record a video of you and your poster on screen while you give the explanation. The videos of all the participants then end up on a shared platform where everyone can watch them.

Presenting your poster online is a completely different experience to a standard poster presentation. Most of the tips you have read in this book will still apply, but there are also a few key differences. Simply sharing an A0 expert poster in the video call and giving an explanation really doesn't work. You'll be bombarding people with an enormous amount of information that is very difficult to read because it looks much smaller on a computer screen than when it's printed out in A0.

If you do decide to share your A0 poster, three things can happen:

1   **They will try to read your poster but won't listen to you.** Because the poster contains too much info that's also too small, they won't listen to anything you say and probably won't make it to the end of your poster either.
2   **They will try to read your poster *and* listen to you.** This doesn't work. They will fail at both and won't remember anything.
3   **They won't read your poster *but will* listen to you**. This is the most workable scenario. If they ignore the poster and listen to you, they are at least getting the information. But what was the point of making the poster then? In this scenario you're actually

giving a short presentation accompanied by a very bad, unreadable slide.

Sharing your standard expert poster online isn't the right approach then. So what should you do instead? There are several options:

1   **Make a pitch poster (highly recommended!).** A pitch poster (see page 90) is the ideal accompaniment to your online pitch. There isn't too much on it so your audience can easily analyse the poster and still listen to you. And because there is less on it, the text is bigger, making it easier to read.

2   **Use animations.** Make the different blocks appear one by one on your poster by using simple animations. At first the audience will only see the image, then the title, then the block with the key message, and then one by one the steps of your story. By making everything appear one step at a time, you keep people focused, they won't be able to rush on ahead, and you won't overwhelm them with information that isn't yet relevant to your talk. Why not build a process step by step? Or let people guess what the third point of your approach is before you show it?

3   **Work with slides.** Forget the poster, and instead use slides to support your short presentation. This of course means you won't be making a scientific poster, but it will be more effective than sharing a large A0 poster.

4   **Use a mix of media.** Presenting online comes with the big advantage that you can do anything your computer allows. You can zoom in on certain parts, show graphs separately so you can look at them in more detail, or even play a video.

3. You're attending a research day

Every university or college has one: a day where researchers introduce their work to each other. It's usually an interdisciplinary event where a biotechnologist explains their research to a psychologist and vice versa. So you can't go into too much detail on one of these days. Once again, the pitch poster is your best bet if you need to create a poster that will strike a chord with everyone. Remember that you're not attending this research day to bombard everyone with jargon or to speak only to other researchers who already know the subject inside out. The whole reason institutions organise research days is to help you get to know *each other* better. And who knows, maybe that biotechnologist and psychologist will end up working on an interesting project together after all.

On a research day, you can take it a step further.

You might consider combining your poster with an activity. Think about how you can help people experience your research. Let's say you're doing research into the anthrax bacteria and anthrax letters that are sent to newspaper editors. Sure, you can explain it on your poster, but you can also put three tables in front of your poster. On the first table, people have to find the anthrax letter among the 50 other letters (just remember to fill it with flour, not real anthrax bacteria). On the second table, they'll analyse the letter and on the third table, they'll draw conclusions that happen to align with your key message.

I'm willing to bet that the participants will never forget your research and that they'll talk about it for years to come. If you ask us, you could also try out this kind of approach at a normal conference, but you may find it a bit stressful. In that case, a research day is the ideal environment. Precisely because it's often a looser, more informal set-up without international guests, and your institution will always be happy to see you take extra initiative to communicate your research.

It really does work

The tips and examples in this book will help you create a poster that stands out from the crowd. Maybe you're not quite comfortable doing things differently from what you're used to. And we get it: creating a poster that looks the same as all the others, full of text and jargon, feels a lot safer. After all, that's what everyone else is doing.

The only way to have real impact, though, is to do things differently. But don't just take our word for it. Find out what other researchers think too.

For example, researcher Willem Verstraeten helped his father – also a researcher – create a pitch poster. His father used the poster at EGU, a conference for geoscientists with 15,000 participants from hundreds of different sub-disciplines, from earth to space sciences. In his own words: 'Never before have I had so much interest in a poster of mine, and I talked so much I was hoarse the next day.'

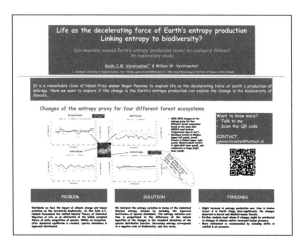

The impact of a pitch poster? 'Never before have I had so much interest in a poster, and I talked so much I was hoarse the next day.'

Or take Ruben Evens. After attending one of our workshops, he decided to rework his expert poster. It went from a fairly typical poster to a much more eye-catching design.

And there are plenty more examples to share. For example:

→ Karlien Van den Bossche, PhD researcher at the University of Antwerp, attended one of our workshops and then at the World Sleep Congress won a Young Investigator Award for her poster.

→ Mieke Van Bockstael, pathologist at Ghent University, took part in a conference in Cologne. She said: 'For the first time, I got several compliments about the layout of my poster. All thanks to The Floor is Yours.'

→ Jan De Pauw, researcher at the Karel de Grote University of Applied Sciences, won first prize at an international conference in Lisbon. He said: 'I really believe that attending one of your workshops was fundamental to my success.'

→ Vincent Joenen, PhD student at Hasselt University: 'A week ago I won my first award for the best poster presentation at a conference. So all credit to you.'

Winning a poster prize is great, and for us personally it's of course nice to get compliments like these, but this isn't what it's really all about. What matters is: it works. In this book we've shown you an approach that really makes a difference.

So make a start, and dare to be different. We're confident that you'll have impact.

Let us know how it goes.
You can reach us at info@thefloorisyours.be.

3 At the conference

Foraging ecology of a heathland specialist reveals the need for change in conservation measurements.

universiteit hasselt | CMK CENTRUM VOOR MILIEUKUNDE

R Evens[1], N Beenaerts[2], N Witters[3] and TJ Artois[1]

Centre for Environmental Sciences, Research Group [1]Zoology: Biodiversity & Toxicology, [2]Environmental biology, [3]Environmental economics. Hasselt University - Campus Diepenbeek, Agoralaan, Gebouw D, BE-3590 Diepenbeek, Belgium

Introduction and goal

Effective conservation in Europe requires **coherent actions** among countries, based on basic **scientific knowledge** concerning **protected species**. Populations of heathland species have dramatically declined over the last century, and nightjars (*Caprimulgus europaeus*) are no exception. <u>**Basic knowledge on nightjar's ranging behaviour or habitat use is still lacking**</u>, and conservation actions are thus inadequately informed

Nightjars are mobile nocturnal insectivores bound to heathlands. Populations have dramatically declined since 20th century due to habitat loss and fragmentation, and they are listed in Annex I of the Bird Directive 2009/147/EEC.

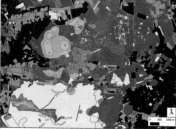

Figure 1: Individuals (one individual = one colour) originating from different parts of the research area use a select number of similar foraging habitats. Kernels: 50% kernels are less transparent than 95% kernels. Habitats: suitable breeding habitat = yellow (Ccut, D, Groa, Hdry & Mmix), suitable foraging habitat = green (Gmed & Rrec) and unsuitable habitat = black (F & Rurb). Sleeping locations of each individual = white stars.

Material and methods

We performed a **long-term radio telemetry study** on **84 nightjars** in Limburg (Belgium) and studied their **ranging behaviour** and **habitat use**.

We used **very High Frequency (VHF) tags** from Biotrack Ltd.: AG393 tailmount-tag; weight 1.45g, (= <3% average weight 72.05g ± 8.33 SE) of adult birds. **Tracking** was done by following a fixed route with 40 area-covering observation points. **Home ranges** were calculated using a kernel density estimator (fixed kernel; fixed multiplier (0,4) limits the number of multi-modal home ranges or inclusions of large unused areas). **Habitat selection** was analysed by comparing kernel placement to available habitat.

Our study area, **Bosland**, an area of 10.000ha in North-eastern Flanders (Belgium). Bosland suffers less intensive farming, contact heathlands of Belgium and the Netherlands. Over 30% of Bosland is included in the Natura 2000 network and contains mosaic landscape consists of coniferous forests (67% of the above), forest (16% above) and only **4% small fragmented heathlands**

Conclusion

We show that conservation of a seemingly well-known species is not straightforward. During the entire breeding period nightjars rely on well-defined habitats, which have not been taken into account in conservation plans so far.
We show that nightjars feed in distant foraging areas, which are dissimilar in habitat composition compared to breeding sites. Maintaining nightjar populations requires not only conservation of breeding areas, but also of foraging sites. With respect to spatial movements and habitat use of nightjars, more consideration has to be given to the regional habitat composition. Hence, implementing scientific knowledge into policy making will ensure long-term survival of nightjars and other species living in associated habitats.

Results

We collected **3105 observations** of 84 radio-tagged nightjars during five breeding seasons (2010-2014). We performed **further analysis** on those birds for which we collected 20 or more observations (n = 52, total = 2753 observations, mean = 53 observations/individual, SE = 19).

Home range size was:
- on average 27.05 hectares for 50% kernels (SE = 18.44ha) and 134.61 hectares for 95% kernels (SE = 91.79ha).
- consistent between years.
- not correlated with the number of observations (50% kernel, R^2 = 0.0028, P = 0.7095; 95% kernel, R^2 = 0.0107, P = 0.4658).
- not influenced by sex (F = 1.049, P = 0.3899)

Habitat choice was not random for both 50% kernels (P < 0.001) and 95% kernels (P < 0.001)

When **nearby to nesting sites** (50% kernel), pine stands (P), wide roads (Groa) or open areas within the forests, such as dunes (D) and heathland fragments (Hdry) were significantly more used than other available habitats. When nightjars moved **away from their nesting grounds** (95% kernel), meadows, extensively grazed grasslands (Gmed) and recreational areas (Rrec) became significantly more important than in the 50% calculations. **Nightjars did not use** urban areas (Rurb) or intensive farmland (F) to forage (figure 2a).

Figure 2: Three (out of seven) individuals tracked for more than one year show consistent home ranges. Kernels: 50% kernels are less transparent than 95% kernels. Habitats: suitable breeding habitat = yellow (Ccut, D, Groa, Hdry & Mmix), suitable foraging habitat = green (Gmed & Rrec) and unsuitable habitat = black (F & Rurb). Sleeping locations of each individual = white stars.

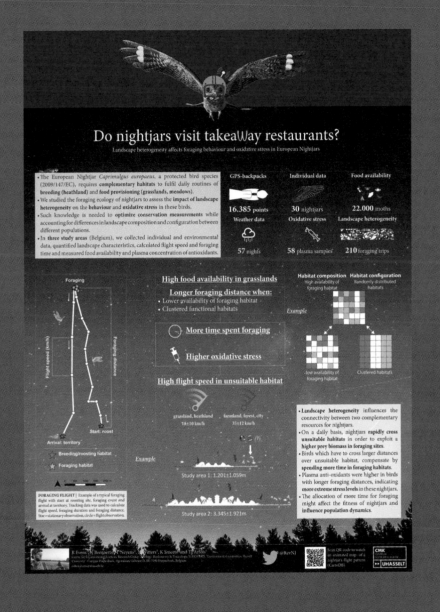

This is the poster Ruben Evens made after the workshop. With the new version he won the Best Early Career Research Award, and the poster was chosen as the best among 180 other participants.

EXTRA TIPS

for poster-session organisers

A few tips especially for poster-session organisers to make researchers' lives a lot easier.

1. Remember that researchers take your word as gospel

They worry that poster-fair organisers will exclude them if they don't strictly adhere to the rules and guidelines.

2. Provide guidance to help them create a good poster

Create a page on your conference or event website with tips on how to create a good poster. You will already have come across a lot of tips in this book, but here are a few more things that we advise organisers to do:

1 **Provide a guideline for the number of words.** For example, a maximum of 400 words, because that's what visitors can read in about five minutes. A word limit is the most valuable piece of advice you can give to researchers. Clearly indicate that it is a guideline and not a requirement, but do provide a specific number. 'Keep the word count low' is too vague. Some researchers think 5,000 words is perfectly fine.

2 **Give good examples**, with comments explaining why you think they are good posters. Then if researchers do decide to go with the 'I'll look at what everyone else did in the past' approach, they will at least be following a good example rather than a design that has been passed around their faculty for the last 12 years. Did you organise a jury or audience award at the previous edition of your event? Then the previous years' winners would certainly be good examples.

3 **Clearly indicate who the conference is aimed at,** and include in the guidelines that researchers should avoid acronyms or jargon that the audience won't understand.

Recommending that researchers read this book is of course also a great idea. **We regularly give poster workshops, online or face to face**. More info about this can be found at thefloorisyours.be. The participants get a lot out of this workshop, and it shows visitors that as an organisation you support clear communication. By organising a workshop six weeks before the conference, you're already getting them involved in your event. And most importantly: your conference will benefit from much better posters.

3. Don't make a template (or at least keep it to a minimum)

You need to guide the researchers to create a good poster, but we don't recommend drawing up a template for the conference. For several reasons:

1 You're crushing their creativity. All the posters at your fair will look the same.
2 Researchers often have their own templates or formats that they prefer to use.
3 I'm of course not familiar with your template and it probably looks absolutely fine. But what if it doesn't? Then your entire poster fair is going to look awful.

If you do decide to provide a template, or your organisation insist you create one, first read the section 'Ignore your institution's template' on page 78 and then follow these simple tips:

1 Give researchers enough freedom. Don't completely fill the middle of the template with dummy text or example blocks. Are you creating a template for a specific conference? Then remember that everyone knows which conference they're attending. So the conference logo and slogan really don't need to appear on every exhibition poster.

Extra tips

2   Include the following:
- →   The header. Make the title big enough (minimum 96 pt). For researchers, it is often more useful for the institution or conference logo to go in the footer rather than the header. This gives them more room to add a clear title.
- →   The footer. The perfect place for logos and contact info.
- →   The colours, with codes.
- →   The right fonts and sizes for titles, subtitles and body text. (See step 10 on page 113 for the right font sizes.)
- →   The maximum number of words. 400 is a good guideline. Encourage less text and the use of images.

So the ideal poster template is relatively empty, which is absolutely fine. Do you want to help your researchers or employees create better posters? Then give them this book. Or ask us to come and give a workshop with a feedback session.

4. Don't ask for an abstract on the poster

A poster is an abstract in itself. It doesn't need an abstract-within-an-abstract. Of course, you can request a summary in advance to include in a book of abstracts or on the conference website, but there's no place for it on a poster. Can't resist making something obligatory? Then make it mandatory to place the key message clearly and prominently on the poster. This is a kind of summary, too, and a much more meaningful one.

5. Provide good lighting, especially in dark rooms

Reading small text in dimly lit rooms is difficult and tiring. There are battery-powered LED lights that are specially made to click onto poster panels. For hundreds of posters, renting these may be quite an investment, but if you have a dark location or a room without any natural light, it's definitely worth it. Even better: find a room with enough daylight. You'll be doing everyone a favour.

6. Share your evaluation criteria

Are you organising a poster contest? Share the evaluation criteria well in advance via the website or in an email to participants. Also let jury members know that the top prize shouldn't necessarily go to the most standard wall-full-of-text poster. Give the jury members examples of posters that meet the criteria, for example from previous years or other events.

7. Organise an audience award

An audience award is an excellent idea, even if you already have a jury award. Perhaps the same poster will win both prizes, but most likely it will highlight some really nice, surprising posters that the jury overlooked for one reason or another. As an organisation, you'll also learn which posters really work. Because ultimately, we create posters for the audience and not for the jury. Right?

Extra tips

8. Allow enough space

There's a lot of foot traffic at a poster fair. For one poster alone you have the presenter, the people talking to them, the people analysing the poster from a distance and the people who are just walking by. If you put one row of posters two metres away from the next row, you'll end up with a human traffic jam. There is no hard and fast rule, but four to five metres between the opposite poster rows is certainly more comfortable. Also allow enough space on either side of a poster so that people can stand around it without completely blocking the next posters in the row.

ABOUT THE FLOOR IS YOURS

Toon and Hans are international experts in science communication. Since setting up The Floor is Yours in 2012, they have trained tens of thousands of researchers in how to clearly communicate their research. From Spain to Finland and from Mexico to South Africa. Has this book made you even more excited to get started? Or are you hoping to get your colleagues on board?

Then book one of our workshops. We'd love to meet you.

Some of the available workshops are listed below. You'll find more workshops on **theflorisyours.be**.

→ **How to stand out with your scientific poster.** The workshop that accompanies this book.
→ **Present with impact.** Learn to present your complex message in a clear and fascinating way.
→ **Pitch your research.** How to pitch your research in 1 to 3 minutes.
→ **Your research in the media.** We help you spread the word about your research.
→ **Writing clear advice or opinion pieces.** You often have to write recommendations or want to write an opinion piece for a magazine. But how do you ensure they're actually read?
→ **Science4Policy.** As a scientist, how can you make sure your research has an impact on policy?

Be sure to also check out the blog, which has loads of useful tips. Subscribe and you'll get a new communication tip every month.

THANK YOU!

This book would not have been possible without the examples and the enthusiastic researchers who wanted to share their stories.

First of all, thank you to the editorial team: five researchers who gave up their valuable time to review the manuscript and provide feedback and ideas. They made sure that the text was as useful as possible and that everything resonated with their experiences. So thank you to Fien Verdoodt (Ghent University), Xena Serifova (KU Leuven), Marlies Maes (Utrecht University), Margot Balcaen (Sciensano) and Renske Bouma (Wageningen University).

Thanks also to the countless researchers who gave permission for us to use their posters or examples in the book. Thank you to Koen Van den Eeckhout, Diana Széliová, Christian Herff, Zsofia Bognar, Ruben Evens, Nicholas Wu, Willem Verstraeten, Thomas Oliver, Linde Proost, Dorde Petrovic, Sanne Van Donink, Elina Vrijsen, Eline Lievens, George Savill, Margot Balcaen, Katleen Wils, Lore Verheyen, Natasha Latouf, Christophe De Coster, Petrović Đorđe, Salvatore Ciano, Franziska Klein, Jeroen Ceyssens, Sohan Sarangi and the SCK CEN research centre.

We hope we haven't forgotten anyone, because we did our very best to track down the correct researcher for each poster and get their permission. That's why we can't say it enough: always put your email address on your poster. This makes it much easier for people (and poster-book authors) to find you. Do you feel like we didn't get the right person after all? Then please let us know at info@thefloor-isyours.be.